Real Faith in Action

Real Faith in Action

*The Demonstration of Nine Principles
that Characterize Authentic Faith*

Curl Oral Hazell

RESOURCE *Publications* • Eugene, Oregon

REAL FAITH IN ACTION
The Demonstration of Nine Principles that Characterize Authentic Faith

Copyright © 2009 Curl Oral Hazell. All rights reserved. Except for brief quotations in critical publications or reviews, no part of this book may be reproduced in any manner without prior written permission from the publisher. Write: Permissions, Wipf and Stock Publishers, 199 W. 8th Ave., Suite 3, Eugene, OR 97401.

Resource Publications
A Division of Wipf and Stock Publishers
199 W. 8th Ave., Suite 3
Eugene, OR 97401
www.wipfandstock.com

ISBN 13: 978-1-60608-781-7

Manufactured in the U.S.A.

All scripture quotations, unless otherwise indicated, are taken from the New King James Version®. Copyright © 1982 by Thomas Nelson, Inc. Used by permission. All rights reserved.

Dedicated in loving memory of my grandparents, George and Rosanna Hazell, who nurtured my brothers, Elvin and Michael, and me in the ways of the Lord from our childhood. This book was made possible in large part because of their godly influence upon my life.

Contents

Preface ix
Acknowledgments xi
Introduction xiii

Principle One	Faith is based on the word of God 1
Principle Two	Faith must be mixed with Righteousness 17
Principle Three	Faith requires doing the "Ridiculous" 31
Principle Four	Faith begins where human ability ends 47
Principle Five	Faith ultimately works toward preparing us for our heavenly home 66
Principle Six	Faith is not nullified by anything, not even death, our last enemy 85
Principle Seven	Faith gives a voice to the dead 93
Principle Eight	Faith sees beyond the present "pleasures" of this life 101
Principle Nine	Faith is the only means whereby we are justified 118

Conclusion 129
Bibliography 131

Preface

IN ORDER TO APPRECIATE the profundity of the principles, it will be important for the reader, while studying them, to keep in mind that they actually cover three essential areas where faith serves to enable us to do the will of God. They are:

1. Empowering us to *become* what God ordained for us to become.
2. Equipping us to *perform* what God commanded us to do.
3. Providing us with confidence to trust God to *obtain* what God promised to give us.

If we are honest, I believe we would admit that in most cases when faith is taught or studied today, almost exclusive attention is given to the role that faith plays in the area of enabling us to acquire the blessings of God. In contrast, the principles of faith, which I am convinced the Holy Spirit strategically laid out for us in Hebrews 11, and which are presented in this book, demonstrate that faith actually serves a three-fold purpose, as outlined above. Overemphasis on any one area while neglecting or minimizing the others, or focus on any two while failing to give equal attention to the third, ultimately leads to worship and service that is not fully pleasing to God. This outcome will always be the same whether our imbalanced approach to faith is due to misunderstanding or deliberate neglect.

As a means to help overcome this problem, the principles present faith as an instrument which God put in the hands of the righteous to accomplish His will in all three areas. Accordingly, in reading this book, it will be important to take note of how faith functioned in each of the three areas in the lives of the past witnesses, because our ability to model the same will be the key to how we will be able to obtain the same testimony they obtained—as having pleased God.

Acknowledgments

To my Lord and Savior, Jesus Christ,
Thank you for saving me, calling me to the ministry, imparting these insights about faith to me, and allowing me the opportunity to share them with many others.

To my mother, Laurene Hazell,
Thank you for insisting that I go to church when I did not want to. Your insistence ensured that I was in the place where I could hear the word of God and be convicted by it, which ultimately led to my salvation. As a result, you have played a major role in inspiring me to write this book.

To the Bishop, Dr. Roderick R. Caesar and the Bethel Ministries,
Thank you for providing quality ministries that equipped me with much of what I have learned in ministry. Your impact on my life has led in large part to the writing of this book.

To Pastor Curtis Thompson,
You were the first to help me realize the gift that God gave me to perform the work of the ministry when I was just a babe in Christ. Your godly influence on me has played a significant role in inspiring me to write this book.

To the Reverend Gregg A. Mast, Ph.D., President of New Brunswick Theological Seminary, and the entire NBTS Family—faculty and students,
Thank you for the invaluable reflection that I received during my years of study in the Master of Divinity Program, and for your continued support even to this day. You have made a significant contribution in inspiring me to write this book. Special thanks also to the Reverend Richard Sturm, Ph.D., my copyeditor, for your tremendous help in this project.

To Andrew Shipe, Ph.D.,
Thank you for your editorial assistance in this project.

To the Agape Family—the people that God entrusted me to lead,
My love and concern for you gave rise to the initial study that culminated in the writing of this book. You have therefore played a major role in this composition. Thank you for your continued love and support for my family and me.

To those who have been praying for me over the years,
Your prayers, many kind words of encouragement, and support have contributed in a major way to inspiring me to write this book.

To Olivia and Nathan, my beloved children,
My prayer for you is that as you grow you will understand faith in its Biblical authenticity, put it into action, and thereby realize the promises of God. I love you!

Last, but by no means least, to my dear wife, my love, Bernadette,
Your role in my life has been invaluable. Thank you for loving me, being by my side, and supporting me in every effort in ministry, including the writing of this book. Thank you for your critique and honest feedback. Love always.

Introduction

THE INSPIRATION

God, by His incredible grace and love, has given us an amazing gift—faith—to be an effective tool in our hands that enables us to serve and please Him. Faith is not only the means whereby we believe God unto salvation, but also what makes it possible for us to trust God to keep us by His grace in fellowship with Him until the day He calls us to the eternal city on high. Moreover, faith is also the substance that enables us to realize the promises of God in our lives. In order for these truths to become reality, however, faith must be appropriated in us. Furthermore, failing to appropriate faith will lead to incalculable destructive consequences in the realm of eternity, as well as to overwhelming despair in this life. For the people of God, while the first risk is avoided, the second—despair in this life—remains a real possibility. This risk ever increases when we are either not thoroughly taught the truth about Biblical faith, or are not taught it correctly. In my observation in recent times, sadly, both factors seem to be contributing to the risk in major ways. As a pastor, therefore, I felt the need, which was no doubt the leading of the Lord, to teach authentic, Biblical faith to those whom I was entrusted to lead in an attempt at least to minimize this danger. Without having this understanding, the flock would be deprived of many of faith's numerous rewards. This likelihood was frightening to consider, especially in light of the mounting uncertainties, doubts, and fears, which many face in today's world.

At least to that point, the culmination of my deep concerns was the Lord's impartation to me of the two-part sermon, "The Principles of Faith" from Hebrews 11. Some time after preaching that message, I felt further impressed of the Lord that this teaching should not be limited in reach to the congregation He had given me oversight of, but it should also be made available to the body of Christ at large. Such prompting was unlike any I had had in relation to any of the other one hundred or so sermons I had preached to that point since becoming a pastor about two years earlier. The truth, as outlined in Hebrews 11 concerning real faith in action, which will be explained in the nine principles comprising the nine chapters of this book, I believe will be life changing to every person of faith who reads it. These principles, as seen in the lives of the heroes of faith that have gone on before us, will inspire faith in every situation of our lives and radicalize our belief in God for everything He has promised us. So buckle up and get ready for an incredible tour of display of hope and trust by many who, against all odds, dared to believe God!

FAITH

Before discussing the principles, an important question must be answered since we are addressing the topic of faith: "Exactly what is faith"? The writer of the book of Hebrews opened chapter 11—the text of focus—with the statement that many quote as a definition of faith: *"Now faith is the substance of things hoped for, the evidence of things not seen."* But was that intended to be a definition though? Instead of being intended to serve as a definition of faith, indications are that the writer perhaps did not have such an intention at all. As noted Biblical scholar, Fred Craddock points out, viewed in context beginning at chapter 10:36–39 through chapter 11:40, the objective may have been to unify the entire discussion of the various acts of faith by describing elements that are at work in any action of faith, and thus the statement was capable of serving as a refrain following each example of faith that would be described.[1] Consequently, while it may be argued that these assertions should be incorporated into any definition of faith, to consider the statement as being a complete definition of faith might go beyond the writer's intent. Perhaps a more accurate assessment of the opening statement about faith in Hebrews 11 then is that it declares some fundamental truths about faith to prepare the reader for the amazing display of faith that many had demonstrated.

It was evidently important to declare these fundamental truths at the outset for as we shall see as we look closely at the amazing courage and beliefs of the heroes, the opening statement serves as a backdrop for the reader to keep in mind in order to fathom how our ancestors endured when at times they must have seemed foolish. To them, there was something tangible and assuring to hold on to in the midst of what must have

---

1. Craddock, "Hebrews," 131.

appeared to others to be situations of impending loss and destruction. That material, the writer declared in his opening statement, was *faith*! In that something was hoped for but was not yet, faith became the substitute in the interim; though they had not yet seen it, because of faith, it was as if they already possessed it.

Having explored what the tactic of the writer of Hebrews may have been by his opening statement, which will help lay the foundation before discussing the principles, a definition of faith is still necessary in order to complete that foundation. As we seek one, we first note that Scripture actually presents faith as a two-dimensional concept. On the one hand, faith is presented as being the entire body of truth that God has revealed to us in Scripture, which we are called to believe and put our trust in.[2] Jude 3 perhaps explains this notion best: *"Beloved, while I was very diligent to write to you concerning our common salvation, I found it necessary to write to you exhorting you to contend earnestly for the faith which was once for all delivered to the saints."* In this passage Jude ardently reminded his readers that God, by His grace, delivered "the faith" in its unadulterated form to the saints. As a result of this reality he encouraged them to fight to uphold that untainted truth in the face of heretics. The faith could not be compromised then or now because only when it is received in its authenticity, and trusted in unconditionally, will it lead a person to salvation through Christ. Other passages that illustrate faith this way include 1 Tim 1:19, 1 Tim 5:8, 1 Tim 6:21, and 2 Tim 3:8.

Upon hearing the declaration that faith must be based on the word of God as the first principle of faith presented in this book does, reference should be noted as simultaneously being made to the first dimension of faith just described. This is because what the word of God reveals to us can be codified as "the faith"; it is the truth that was given to us as a gift of God, it is what we have trusted in, and it is what has led us to salvation in Christ. While the term *faith* is more widely used to describe the act of believing and trusting in God, therefore, this other usage of the term in Scripture must be understood as always being at the heart of the term in general because it is indeed "the faith"—the entire revealed body of truth—that we have been called to believe if we are to activate the purposes of God in our lives. So while principles 2–9 highlight the second, more popular dimension of the term *faith*, the first dimension will always

---

2. Unger, *Bible Dictionary*, 396.

be kept in view and at times will be alluded to throughout the survey of the principles. But just before we delve into the principles we will briefly discuss and define faith in terms of the primary dimension—believing and trusting in God for His promises contained in His word.

Just as we understand the traditional dimension of faith—the revealed body of truth—to be a gift from God since humanity received it by revelation and not by construction, the second dimension must also be conceptualized as being a gift from God as well. Although exercising faith in God requires believing and trusting on our part, understanding the truth about faith as being a gift from God will eliminate the notion that faith is a human achievement, which can lead to both a false sense of pride in assuming to possess the ability to procure the promises of God, and a superiority or inferiority complex surrounding one's perceived measure of faith, depending on one's disposition.

Renowned theologian, Stanley Grenz provides an insightful overview of faith that I think will be beneficial to make mention of to help us appreciate faith as being a gift of God.[3] He highlights three essential components of faith that work in harmony to secure the final goal of bringing into fruition the will of God. They are: *knowledge, assent,* and *trust.* Although Grenz discussed these components from the standpoint of faith working in us unto salvation, the three must be recognized as being at work in any appropriation of faith to bring to pass any of the promises of God. Brief analysis of each should readily demonstrate what has been asserted thus far regarding faith being freely and generously handed down to us by God. *Knowledge* speaks of the information about the promises of God. This information is contained in Scripture and we learn of it when we hear the word of God (Rom 10:17). And clearly Scripture is God's gift to us so that we can claim no credit for its composition. Thus in the initial stage of faith's working in us, human ineptness is exposed to remind us not to be haughty but grateful that we have faith.

Assent involves intellectual acknowledgement that the knowledge that has been received is truth to the point that it is now believed. It is one thing to hear the word of God, but another thing to believe it. Many hear the word, but very few believe it. While it is true that in order to do this it will require a decision on one's part, the fact still remains that the only reason why we have the *capacity* to make such a decision is because of God's grace, which hardly any rational person would deny as being a

3. Grenz, *Theology,* 408–411.

gift of God. The willingness or unwillingness to make the decision rests with us, but the *capacity* to make it was given to us as a gift. This is why the apostle Paul said, "*For by grace you have been saved through faith, and that not of yourselves; it is the gift of God, not of works, lest anyone should boast*" (Eph 2:8–9). Not only is this true about salvation, but also concerning any of the numerous other promises of God. In *assent*, therefore, it is also evident that faith is a gift of God.

Trust, the third component of faith, completes faith in that it involves committing one's life to the knowledge that was received and acknowledged to be truth. Again, it might appear that this aspect of faith can support the erroneous notion that faith is a human endeavor instead of a gift of God. But while it is true that *trust* requires that we follow through with the radical act of performing what we have acknowledged to be truth from the knowledge we receive, because commitment involves total reliance on another, namely, God, to bring about the desired outcome, such as salvation, healing, or peace, and the one who trusts has absolutely no power to secure it, the *trust* component of faith actually call attention to the fact that faith is a gift. We *trust,* not in ourselves, but in God, who afforded us this amazing privilege, which we could not earn. The three therefore, *knowledge, assent,* and *trust* all support the truth that faith is a gift of God. Thus, in any act of faith, works-righteousness is excluded; but grace—a free gift of God—enjoys prominence because it is the means whereby we receive faith, and for that we should be thankful!

As a caution, the placement of *trust* as being the third component of faith is not to be understood as being a result of ranking so that it is the least important of the three. The danger of this is that one might be inclined to think that the more intellectual one is, that is, the more knowledge of the word one has and ability to appropriate that knowledge as being truth, the more faith one will have. Such thinking leads to elitism. This goes against the spirit of the message that the writer of Hebrews wanted to convey. The heart of the message conveyed in Hebrews 11 is that the Ancients demonstrated remarkable *trust* and hope in God's faithfulness (see Heb 11:1). In essence, therefore, the *trust* component of faith is what is highlighted in the roll call of faith, more so than *knowledge* and *assent*. This being said, the importance of *knowledge* and *assent* should also be emphasized because one can put remarkable *trust* in God for something that God does not intend to give the individual, for one reason or another, including because that thing might oppose God's will in general or His plan for the individual. This scenario is most likely to happen when one does not *know* the *truth* contained in God's word.

Of course, in order for a gift to benefit the one who receives it, it will have to be put to good use. The same is true about faith, it will not benefit us unless we put it to use and exercise it. This is precisely what the past witnesses did; in other words, they had no advantage over us with respect to receiving faith for "*God shows no partiality*" (Acts 10:34); the same faith that they received through grace has been imputed to us as well. If we exercise our faith as they did we will also experience similar triumphs as they enjoyed, for it is God's desire that we do so, which is why He graced us with this precious gift. As we take the journey through the principles to see how our ancestors utilized this priceless gift, then, it is hoped that we will be inspired to utilize it as well.

Returning to our quest for a working definition of faith, we observe that The New Unger's Bible Dictionary provides a simple definition which also encompasses the three components just described: faith is "belief or trust—especially in a higher power. The fundamental idea in Scripture is steadfastness and faithfulness."[4] The author goes on to outline two key elements that are intrinsic to such belief or trust. Faith is first intellectual in that one's intellect must agree with revealed truth, that is, no matter how foolish it may seem, as long as Scripture declares something to be so, one must accept it. Secondly, and even more importantly, faith is also moral in that it is not enough simply to believe, but such belief must move beyond the intellect to the "practical submission of the entire man to the guidance and control of such truth.[5] In other words, one must believe to the extent that he or she will put his/her life on the line if that is what that belief mandates.

For our purposes, then, just before advancing to the principles, we put it all together—the fundamental truths as laid down in the opening statement of Hebrews 11, what we have gleaned from the discussion by Grenz, and the definition provided by Unger. *Faith is unwavering belief or trust in God that is characterized by intellectual assent to His revealed truth to such an extent that one is willing to yield his or her life to the guidance of that truth.* "Faith is the substance of things hoped for, the evidence of things not seen" (Heb 11:1—last statement only). Having now introduced the subject of faith—its two dimensions, a working definition, and the key elements noted in the opening statement of Hebrews 11, we now turn to the principles.

4. Unger, *Bible Dictionary*, 396.
5. Ibid.

Principle One

Faith is based on the word of God

"By faith we understand that the worlds were framed by the word of God, so that the things which are seen were not made of things which are visible."

Heb 11:3

Appropriately, this is the first principle of faith that we see in Hebrews 11. In the opening statement of declaration about faith in the chapter we learn that *"faith is the substance of things hoped for."* A key notion here is that faith gives us confidence to hope. Equally important to understand in conjunction with this is that faith likewise has its foundation in something else that gives us assurance—the word of God. The apostle Paul put it this way: *"So then faith comes by hearing, and hearing by the word of God"* (Rom 10:17). Faith is thus belief in what God has revealed to us in His word. So while it is true that it is faith that gives us confidence to believe, it should also be evident that this confidence ultimately comes from the word of God, which illustrates that faith is based on the word of God.

This truth is established in Heb 11:3, I believe, to demonstrate that though it was by faith the elders obtained a good testimony, their ultimate confidence and hope was in the word of God. In that verse it is affirmed *"that the worlds were framed by the word of God."* This statement of affirmation illustrates the importance of the word of God for faith on two levels. To understand the first level, we must take note of two things. First, it is evident that it is by faith we have come to accept the account of Genesis concerning the creation of the universe. After all, no human being was there to witness it, but by faith we understand it, believe it, and accept it! The next is that such faith is not without foundation but its foundation is on the word of God which is the *only* means by which we can know for sure how the worlds were created. Accordingly, concerning the manner in which our universe came into being, the faith to believe in divine creation can only be based on the word of God. The same is also true about everything else we believe about God; faith to believe can only be based on the word of God since it is where we discover the truth about God. So, on the first level, the statement of affirmation in Heb 11:3 demonstrates the importance of the word of God for faith by establishing it as the sole basis for faith. On the second level, in that the worlds were created by the word of God alone, confidence is provided to base our belief in that word because it has proven to contain sufficient power to accomplish anything it proclaims, even to create something out of nothing, including the universe! How appropriate, the universe is the beginning of the created world which we see; and if it was created by the word of God alone, we should be assured that everything else that is created within it is subject to the power and authority of the same word, giving us confidence to rest our hope in it. Consequently, we can boldly believe and trust God for all the promises contained in His word. Thus in every way the word of God proves to be the sure foundation upon which our faith is based.

The primacy of the word as being the basis for faith simply cannot be overstated. Often what we consider to be faith is nothing more than presumption. Presumption in that we choose to believe God for something and hold all confidence in the reality of that thing, even against all odds; meanwhile, the only basis for believing God for that thing is our own word emanating from our fleshly desires. When this happens, what might appear to be amazing faith, in that someone might display sustained belief in a hope in the face of indications to the contrary, is often pseudo-faith, since the basis for *true* faith is absent, which is the word of God. As a result, the lesson for every reader of the examples of faith in Hebrews 11 is clearly laid out early in the chapter: the Ancients accomplished amazing feats through faith because their faith was founded on the word of God; and although every reader is expected to be inspired, they should also understand that the same must be true for them if they expect to accomplish anything by faith.

Of course this leads to the obvious question of how one can know the word of God in order to believe it with confidence. As straightforward as it may seem, this is perhaps one of the most puzzling questions that every believer wrestles with. On the one hand, we seek to know how to discern the truth of what the written word of God says. The perfect illustration of how miserably we have failed in this endeavor is to take note of the many contradicting interpretations we hear surrounding various portions of Scripture that have even shaped denominations and created divisions in the body of Christ, indicating this is by no means any simple matter. On the other hand, there is the constant struggle to know the unwritten word of God, which God speaks into our spirits but which must conform to the written word, such as whom one should marry, or if one should look for a new job and quit the present one. What God is saying in either instance—written or unwritten—must be known beyond the shadow of a doubt and once known, be believed, trusted, and acted upon without doubting or wavering, and it will come to pass. This is how faith works in us. Of course, knowing this is good, but it still leaves unanswered the question of how we can know the word of God so we can believe it.

THE WRITTEN WORD OF GOD

Just as I will do in the case of knowing the unwritten word of God, I begin by stating that we can only know the truth of the written word of God based on this premise which we accept by faith: the author of the book—the Holy Spirit—has to guide us in that truth. Jesus, while preparing for His ascension, comforted his disciples that *". . . when He, the Spirit of truth, has come, He will guide you into all truth . . ."* (John 16:13). The word of God is truth as stated in John 17:17, but we need the illumination of the Holy Spirit to impart it to our hearts because we are not able to comprehend it with our minds alone, since the word is spirit and it is life, thus requiring the Spirit to quicken it to our hearts (John 6:63). But this does not exempt us from our responsibility to seek diligently to learn what the word says in order for the Holy Spirit to help us recall this knowledge when needed and to give us correct interpretation through various means, which we will discuss below. As a result, the key to how we can know what God says to us in His written word is to begin with the obvious: we must become students of the word of God!

Being created as intelligent beings in God's own image, we humans are expected by God to utilize our minds to study that we may learn. Studying happens on different levels and where learning the word of God is concerned, the beginning point is simply to read it. The word of God is rich beyond human comprehension to supply hope for literally every situation in our lives. The devil, because he is aware of this, utilizes his influence on the world and our flesh in making every attempt to keep us from reading it. When we do not read it, however, we actually give the Holy Spirit very little to work with in being able to illuminate that word to our hearts that we might embrace it by faith to achieve results. For this reason, we must become deliberate in setting aside substantial amounts of time on a daily basis for reading and meditating on the word.

In our present visual, entertainment society, by and large, we have become disinterested in reading on a whole. Tragically, this disinterest has trickled down to include the believer's approach to the word of God, which leads to our over dependence on others to read and study the word for us. This attitude signifies irresponsibility not only with matters pertaining to this life but also those of eternity. When we do not read the word for ourselves we make ourselves easy prey to false teachings that result from others' uninformed interpretations or their willful use of the word to manipulate others. Regardless of the reason for their error, the effects can be destructive. On the one hand, we can develop a false hope in which to put our trust, while on the other hand, we may be deprived of knowing the truth of the word so that we can believe it.

In seeking to know what God's word says, therefore, we must become students of the word and in being students we must be diligent to read and meditate on the word both regularly and substantially so that the Holy Spirit can give us understanding (see 2 Cor 3). Also, because we desire the Holy Spirit's guidance, it is also expedient that we pray earnestly, asking the Lord to give us understanding of His word, even before beginning to read. This is surely a prayer that, we can be confident the Lord will answer. He longs to see us live in the light of His word; and to see His children reaching out to Him for understanding of His word is something He delights in and will reward. To pray also demonstrates to God (and to us) that we do not rely on our own intellect alone to comprehend the word, and praying puts us in the mode of openness to the Spirit to impart His word. Prayer is also vital for preparation of reception of the word in every other mode in which it goes forth, such as in preaching and teaching. This is crucial so that the Lord can give us discernment to detect the truth and any departure from it, no matter how subtle.

The importance of prayer should also be evident when utilizing study aids such as Study Bibles, Concordances, Bible Commentaries, and Bible Dictionaries. In prayer, the Holy Spirit's guidance should be sought to help detect whenever these resources misinterpret Scripture. In addition, these study aids should be employed only following the advice of spiritual leaders for as important as they may be, it is important to remember that they are not inspired writings in the way Scripture is. They sometimes contradict each other and basically reflect someone else's interpretation or particular denominations' persuasions, which may or may not be correct. Prayer and advice of spiritual leaders become critical as a result so that false hopes or misled beliefs are not embraced. This being said, the fact still remains that the use of study aids are vital for our understanding of the word. Study aids are especially useful for interpreting Scripture in context—chapter, book, the whole of Scripture, history, and theology. Honoring the context is essential for us to practice, since failure to do so may lead to false ideologies about God that have severe consequences. There is no doubt, I believe, the Holy Spirit utilizes these methods of interpretation to help illuminate His truth to our hearts. The Holy Spirit is the one who gifted teachers to teach His word, and it is remarkable and noteworthy that many of those teachers have labored and do continue to labor arduously to prepare study aids to help others understand it also. The truth of the matter is, whether we acknowledge it or not, to deny the need for these tools is tantamount to denying the need for teachers in the body of Christ.

There is one final dimension that must be mentioned in considering someone as a true and responsible student of the word of God. This is the need to engage in some level of systematic study of the word. Beyond personal devotional reading, this is disciplined study in the "classroom" setting where there are teachers and fellow students. This type of environment of study promotes in depth reflection, more critical thinking, and consideration of other views. Especially important is that it helps to prevent being carried away in pursuit of the fulfillment of erroneous private interpretations that can lead to devastating results to such an extent as giving rise to cults and leading multitudes astray from the faith. This level of study is thus a vital component in the overall discipline of becoming a conscientious student of the word.

Engaging in systematic study of the word will require different levels of commitment and even sacrifice from each individual based on a variety of factors. One major factor is that of our calling in the body of Christ, such as to the pastorate, teaching Sunday school, leading a small Bible study group, or even to witness to others one-on-one. Regardless of the category, this level of study is a requirement for every person of faith. The level of study should be determined by the type of preparation needed for the particular calling one is preparing for. One must be responsible to do this, taking into account it is not only necessary for personal understanding for faith but also to help others understand for their faith. Even if one is a regular attendee of a Sunday school class or mid-week Bible Study, this could meet the requirement for some; but once again, the type of calling should determine what is necessary. I will also add that there may be some who may not be preparing for any particular calling but will decide to study at the highest level, such as Seminary. In cases like this many often prepare for callings that they might not be aware of during the time of study, but when the time for fulfilling the calling arrives, the necessity for the study becomes evident. At any rate, it should be clear that there is a mandatory requirement for every child of God that some level of systematic study be a part of their Christian walk.

Too many in the body of Christ seem to think they do not need teaching in the word beyond the Sunday morning message and listening to teachings on the radio, television, or the Internet. This is evident from the fact that churches are generally crowded during Sunday morning worship yet only a very small percentage of those same worshipers attend Sunday school and mid-week Bible study. Some may argue that it is not that they do not see the need for such study but there are too many obstacles such as work schedule and fatigue that hinders them from participating. These excuses may seem legitimate at first but when we take into account what is at stake, we just have to acknowledge that all they are, are excuses. We must be deliberate to do whatever is necessary if we consider ourselves to be responsible students of the word, which we must be if we desire to know the truth of the word of God in order to have true faith in it.

In conclusion, then, if we desire to understand the written word of God we must first seek the guidance of the Holy Spirit in it by first asking Him in prayer to illuminate the word to our hearts. Then we must be diligent in reading and meditating on the word regularly and substantially on a daily basis. The use of study aids must also be utilized to help clarify those areas which we find difficult to understand. Finally, we must engage in some level of systematic study involving teachers and fellow students for critical reflection. To do these things may not mean we will become scholars, which, by the way, is not the goal; it will ensure however that we give ourselves the best chance of knowing and understanding the word. Indeed, we do not simply give ourselves a good chance but we can be confident that in making such an effort, the Lord will reward us for it by giving better and better understanding of His word. Consequently, in becoming responsible students of the word, we can have full assurance that we can boldly rest our faith on something sure, which is the word of God in its correct interpretation.

THE UNWRITTEN WORD OF GOD

As should have been noticed in the discussion above concerning understanding the written word of God, it should also be noticed that the same is also true in the case of knowing the unwritten word of God: it is very rarely an instant process. This process too will require both patience and discipline. Consider this, the issues that are usually at stake, such as whether to marry a particular individual or whether to take up a different city of residence, are ones which most would agree are by no means decisions to be rushed into. Rather, most would take the time to research carefully and ponder these actions that can bring joy to their lives or ruin. Continuing in this same approach, it should be reasonable to think that if seeking God's will on these matters is a part of the decision-making process then, care should be taken to ensure that what one thinks one hears from God is indeed what God has said. Furthermore, it is important to keep in mind that when seeking answers there will be many "voices" that respond—voices from within, from others, or even from the devil. As a result, we must be disciplined in observing certain safeguards to ensure that amid all the voices that are heard, God's voice will be clearly and convincingly discerned. Understandably, in this present "microwave" society in which we live where everyone has to have everything yesterday, this is not a popular approach. Still, we must remember that we should be disciplined in our pursuit of Christ. This discipline should characterize every area of our Christian walk, including seeking to know God's word and will on every issue in our lives.

Bearing in mind God will never speak a word which contradicts Scripture, in seeking to know the unwritten word which He speaks, I believe the starting point must be always to observe key principles from the written word. These will serve as guiding lights to prevent us from stumbling into the darkness of "a word" that is contradictory to what God has already revealed in Scripture. Of course, if one is to observe something, it is expected that one must first be familiar with it. In other words, where Scripture is concerned, one must be taught in it. This takes us back to the previous discussion of how one comes to know and understand the truth of the written word and how obtaining the ability to do so will require becoming a responsible student of the word. The two therefore go hand in hand—the written and the unwritten word— because the Lord uses both means to speak to us.

Some of the principles to be observed from the written word when seeking to discern the unwritten should be apparent. For example, if one is considering marrying someone and needs confirmation from the Lord; among other things, it is important to know that we are not to be *"unequally yoked together with unbelievers"* (2 Cor 6:14). The yoke was a device used in farming to keep two animals linked together for plowing to prevent one from walking in a different direction from the other so that the two, going in the same direction, were able to accomplish the farmer's goal of plowing the field in a uniformed fashion. Likewise, in marriage, a believer should not marry an unbeliever, no matter how many other similarities they may share because there are guaranteed to be problems because of the faith. Now this does not mean Scripture in any way advises divorcing one's spouse because he or she is an unbeliever. To the contrary, Scripture advises the believing spouse to win over the unbelieving spouse with holy conduct (1 Pet 3:1). Nevertheless, the scenario should only occur in cases where both persons were unbelievers, they got married, then one became a believer and the other did not. But for a believer to take the risk of marrying an unbeliever because one thinks one can help the other become saved is clearly to go against the advice of Scripture. It is simply not our job to guarantee anyone's salvation; nor is it wise for us to frustrate our own. When seeking God's will concerning whom to marry then, by utilizing this principle, a major portion of the answer should immediately be known.

Another principle, which is crucial to keep in mind and which will do us a world of good in this process, is to remember that we should *"Be anxious for nothing"* (Phil 4: 6). When faced with difficult situations that need answers, we should never become frantic and make rash decisions before waiting to hear from God. The Scripture continues, *"... but in everything by prayer and supplication, with thanksgiving, let your requests be made known to God."* Accordingly, when we face opposition on our jobs, for example, we ought not to panic and quit or to even begin to look for another, unless we have sought the Lord for direction. No matter what's going on around us, we must practice to first *"Be still"* and know that God is God (Ps 46:10). This guiding principle reminds us that no matter the situation we face, the proper course of action for the child of God is to always cultivate the peace of God, knowing that the God of the entire universe and beyond is on our side, making us *"more than conquerors"* because He fights our battles and allows us to plunder the spoils (Rom 8:37).

There are also many other similar guiding principles to help us in the quest to know God's response to our questions. The Holy Spirit will remind us of them when He speaks to us to give us assurance of the validity of the answers He will give. This is where we must recall that part of the Spirit's mission of being responsible for guiding us into all truth (John 16:13), just as we saw in the case of the written word. So it is evident that even before God has to speak a direct word in response to our inquiries on any matter, we should already know a major portion and maybe the entire answer, or at least be primed to receive a clear answer, just by observing these guiding principles. Still, I am aware, this does not satisfy in answering the question of how we can fully discern the word which God speaks into our spirits.

As we move to this all important discussion, I would like to highlight a key word from the previous statement that should be noted as being the objective at hand, which is "how" we can know what God is saying. In other words, the focus will be kept on "how" we discern what God is saying and not on "what" God is saying. The reason being: what God says will obviously depend on what God is saying at a particular time to a particular individual, which is clearly impossible to determine here. That will be something for the individual to know at those times. On the other hand, learning how to discern when God speaks is something we hope to achieve at this time in order to apply such understanding to those moments when we need to know the "what" which God speaks. In accomplishing this, we also hope to obtain confidence that the "what" that we believe we hear from God is indeed the authentic word of God, so we can believe it with all assurance. As we set out to achieve that ultimate goal, I will utilize two examples, once again from Scripture, where we will see two great concepts at work. If we walk in them I am confident we should find hearing from God to be something that happens with clarity to the point where it will seem as if we were hearing another human being speak to us in an audible voice!

ASCENDING THE TOWER

The first example is found in the Old Testament book of Habakkuk. The book may be summarized as a report of a couple of question and answer sessions between Habakkuk the prophet and God, and a concluding prayer by the prophet. It opens with a cry to God from the prophet asking how long he needed to cry out concerning sin in the land of Judah—and the Lord not hear nor do anything about it. Following the prophet's recital of the atrocities, to which God seemed to turn a blind eye, the Lord responded. But God's response was shocking to the prophet: God was determined to use a nation more wicked than Judah to be the instrument of His judgment upon Judah. This gave rise to yet another question posed to God by the prophet: how can you, being holy, behold the wicked devouring someone more righteous than himself? Following this next question, the posture assumed by the prophet in anticipation of the answer becomes the focus for our first observance of how we can likewise place ourselves in a strategic position to hear clearly what God is saying to us.

The prophet spoke within himself, purposing to stand on a tower to watch to see what God would say and how he would respond when answered and corrected. No doubt this was only symbolic and not to be taken as a literal positioning. Yet it is interesting because a tower signifies a fortress for defense; but against whom or what was Habakkuk defending himself or his possessions? That we will explore a little later, but for now I would like to note that the primary purpose of standing his watch upon a tower, even if only figuratively, was for clarity of sight and sound. It was a strategic measure taken by the prophet, which allowed him to hear with precision what God would say. Keeping in mind we seek to know *how* we can know what God is saying, the prophet's example in anticipation of answers should be of great help to us in our personal quests for the same. From his example it should be clear: being determined to place oneself in the *best* position to receive unobstructed answers from God is perhaps the most important step to take to ensure receiving those answers.

The scenario may be conceptualized as involving a person receiving tutoring in mathematics; as the tutor is tutoring, the student is preoccupied in watching a football game on television. The lack of effectiveness, not of the tutor's efforts but of the ability of the student to grasp the concepts that he is being taught at such a moment, is obvious. If nothing else, it will certainly not be as effective as if the student had given his undivided attention and focus to receiving guidance from the instructor. As a matter of fact, the approach of this student raises the question of whether he/she was truly interested in receiving help in the first place. Now as we think of our pursuits for answers from God, I think we should ask similar questions of ourselves. For example, in seeking answers from God, am I interested enough to put myself in the best position to hear clearly from God; and, do I care enough to do so? Obviously Habakkuk was interested enough and cared enough to do what was necessary, and now hopefully we will learn from his example so the same can be said of us.

Also of major significance to Habakkuk's position is the dimension of defense that it allowed, which I alluded to above. We literally have to picture the place of hearing from God as one in which there will be much opposition to our reception of the answer. Many distractions and preoccupations will work to interfere with our reception of the word of God into our hearts. This means we have to incorporate a defensive positioning as a part of our strategy to receive from Him, a positioning which the tower affords. By standing upon a tower, we are able to spot from afar intruders into our hearing airspace and defend ourselves and our blessings from them. For example, in the case of being tutored in math, the simple defense move is to turn off the television. While that might sound simple enough, such is not the case for the one who has not ascended to the top of the tower. Even more challenging are those difficult distractions that are really vices. Despite their obviousness, we tend to find little power within to fight them off. These may include relationships that pull us away from seeking the Lord or even long work hours that cause us to be so mentally fatigued that we cannot hear clearly. Then above all, there are those not so obvious distractions such as being too busy in the work of the Lord, which is an innocent and noble action, yet unwise because in so doing we are unable to hear even the One who we claim to work for. Being in a defensive position, highly seated upon the tower, therefore, is of great importance if expect to hear clearly when God speaks.

Again, Habakkuk undoubtedly spoke of positioning himself upon a tower only as being analogous of the type of posture he assumed in order to hear from God, and we likewise must adopt the same mentality if we are to be as successful as he was. To convey the concept in real every day examples would include measures such as increasing one's prayer life, including regular fasts periods into our spiritual lives, meditating on the word more, and being attentive in church, recognizing that God can speak a word to our situations at any moment in the service. In assuming these "tower" positions, we allow the Holy Spirit the best chance of being heard when He speaks to us. Possibly, this suggested solution to the problem of how to hear from God might not sound like the one many had hoped for; nonetheless, I am convinced it is the one we need to hear because there is a growing problem of a lack of discipline in our pursuits of the things of God and many of us have succumbed to it. Furthermore, the warning from the beginning should be recalled: hearing from God is most often not an instant process.

One final observation from Habakkuk is that not only did he speak of the position he assumed, but he also spoke of a frame of mind which he obviously realized was necessary to have when desiring to hear from God. This was important, since the answer could have been unfavorable to him, which indeed it was, because it came in the form of a rebuke. Consequently, in addition to watching to see what God would say to him, the prophet also made mention of preparing himself to give an answer when he was corrected. Habakkuk was realistic in understanding that because he himself was not God to have known all things, there existed the possibility of his going too far either in his line of questioning to God or even in the act of questioning itself, thus creating the likelihood that God might need to correct him. This acknowledgement by the prophet highlights an important aspect to the "tower" positioning: one has to be prepared for an unfavorable answer. Like the favorable answer, an unfavorable response is an answer, which is what we seek from the Lord. In fact, looking back at our past, if we are honest, we will admit that in most cases when we fell flat on our faces the reason was not because we did not hear from God; rather, when we did, we did not like the answer He gave, so we proceeded to do the opposite, at which time we encountered trouble. Sometimes the answer may even be to wait, but it is an answer nonetheless, and we must be prepared to receive it. If we truly desire to hear from God, like Habakkuk, we must be prepared for the potentially unfavorable response, or we might just miss the answer altogether, no matter how loudly God speaks it to us.

Conversely, once we have ascended the tower and have a clear view and a defensive positioning with respect to the answer as it approaches and we are prepared to receive any answer the Lord chooses to give, even the unfavorable one, knowing it will always be the answer we need to hear, then I am convinced we can be assured of receiving His response.

Remember, part of the Holy Spirit's mission today is to guide us into all truth, so we can have confidence in His faithfulness to do so. All God requires is that we do our part in positioning ourselves in the place where we can hear what He is saying to us, since He will surely speak. As in the case of Habakkuk where the answer was heard following the steps he took, as he reported, *"Then the Lord answered me and said"* (Hab 2:2), we can also be sure to hear the answer which God speaks to us. This assurance comes as a result of the confidence we have by faith in the word of God. Faith gives us this insight concerning the correct "tower" positioning to assume, in order to hear from God. Habakkuk also declared, *"the just shall live by his faith"* (Hab 2:4). It is by faith we walk in the word expecting to hear from God because it contains numerous promises of the same such as: *"It shall come to pass that before they call, I will answer; and while they are still speaking, I will hear"* (Isa 65:24). We can therefore have confidence that once we are in the right place—upon the tower—we will hear from God when He speaks!

Although our focus is primarily on how we can position ourselves to hear from God and not necessarily on how God speaks, I think it would be helpful at this juncture to discuss briefly some of the ways in which God does speak. This is important so that when we are on the tower we will be on the lookout with *trained* eyes for any means by which God might choose to give the answer. Of course, one method is by His word because God can use a variety of passages of Scripture to speak to us in a number of ways. Next has to be prayer. During prayer and occasional fasting we speak to God, but even more importantly in the process we also put ourselves in a great position to listen, to hear God speak into our spirits. God also speaks through other means such as the preached word, through counsel, or even during normal conversation with others. God uses dreams and visions, although He may not speak through all dreams, as dreams are natural occurrences frequently experience during sleep. God sometimes uses circumstances to get our attention, which may include moments of pleasure and times of trouble. God also speaks to us in a host of other ways which we must be careful not to miss; indeed, God spoke through a donkey on one occasion (Num 22:28–30)! God might speak through any means He chooses at any time. We may not even conceive of these means now, but if we position ourselves upon the tower, we will not miss His voice but will hear it clearly.

COME CLOSER

There is one other dimension I would like to add to the discussion of how we can hear and discern the word of God which He speaks into our spirits. I speak of paying close attention to our proximity to the Lord. This may seem obvious, and it should be; yet as it is in the case of many other apparent things, with this we also tend to encounter difficulty in motivating ourselves to pursue it. James 4:8 says, *"Draw near to God and He will draw near to you."* Here we have a promise from the written word that essentially also serves as a guarantee of how we can hear the unwritten. The basis upon which we can have this assurance lies simply in the logic that God does not want us to draw near to Him for nothing. He genuinely wants to have an intimate relationship with us and to aid us in every area of our lives. One of those areas is in giving us direction—which requires that God speak to us, and drawing closer to God will ensure that we hear those words.

To give clarity to the directive of drawing closer to God to allow Him to draw closer to us, James used the analogy of the marriage relationship (Jas 4:4). He made it emphatically clear that friendship with the world drives us farther away from God because such unfaithfulness will produce the same result as committing adultery in a marriage in that it creates separation. On the other hand, if we expect God to draw closer to us, the same will be required as is required in a marriage—we must put forth an effort to draw closer to God just as one spouse must draw closer to the other if he or she expects intimacy in the relationship. Now we know that *"God so loved the world that He gave His only begotten Son..."* (John 3:16) which means God has already done His part in attempting to come close to us. But in addition to God's effort to come close to us, there is that part which depends on us to make it happen, which is what James spoke of in this passage. If we expect God to draw closer to us, therefore, we must also draw closer to Him.

The benefits to this action as it relates to hearing from God should be readily apparent on two fronts. First, the closer one is to the source of a sound, the clearer and louder one will hear it. Secondly, an intimate relationship with God is needed, just as two persons' level of understanding of each other increases in a marriage with increased intimacy. Concerning the first case, one of the causes of our frustration of not being able to hear God's voice is simply because we are too far from Him! We expect to hear when He speaks to us yet we fail to take the simple step to ensure being able to do so, which is to draw closer to Him. Remember, we operate from the premise by faith that God does speak to us because He promised to guide us into all truth by His Spirit (John 16:13). The issue therefore is by no means how to prompt God to speak but how to hear Him when He does speak, and drawing closer to Him will ensure that we hear Him when He does.

In terms of intimacy, the benefits can also be seen in helping us hear God. Have you ever noticed that the longer a couple has been married, provided the relationship is a loving one, each spouse tends more and more to think like the other? This is because the two are so intimate that one understands how the other thinks to the extent that if questioned separately on a variety of topics the answers are likely to be very close and at times even identical. As this correlates to our relationship with God and our ability to hear Him, the advantage is amazing when comparing being in close fellowship with Him as opposed to when someone does not enjoy such closeness with the Lord. Because one is so close to the Lord as to "know" and to "understand" God's thoughts on an issue, often God's answer is immediately known because we already "know" how God thinks due to our intimacy with Him. Of course, in speaking of knowing how God thinks we speak only of that portion of His thoughts which God chooses to allow us to understand, since He is God and there will always be an infinite gap between His thoughts and ours. Yet spontaneously knowing His answers to our questions at times is precisely what can happen when we are close to Him, because when we are close to Him, what the apostle Paul spoke of will be at work in us: we will *"have the mind of Christ"* (1 Cor 2:16). Also, even if we do not already "know" what God is thinking on an issue, because we are intimate with Him we can discern which of the many voices we might hear is actually His. Knowing Him will help us eliminate the imitators. Jesus emphasized this truth in the metaphor of the sheep of the flock of the Good Shepherd (John 10:1–5). The sheep of the fold will not respond to the voice of strangers because they know the voice of the Good Shepherd, who is the Lord.

Drawing closer to God therefore, among other things, is beneficial in "sharpening" our ears to hear when God speaks to us. Efforts to draw near to God include the same things we discussed above in the "tower positioning" such as increasing our prayer life, fasting, meditating on the word, and practicing other spiritual disciplines. In addition, as James emphasized, we must be faithful in following Christ and not be unfaithful in flirting with the world. The closer we come to Him, the better we can hear His every word. Accordingly, our goal should be to get close enough to Him to hear even His whisper, even when in a crowded, noisy room in which there are many other voices speaking to us! God speaks loudly enough for us to hear Him but our positioning will determine if we actually will and thereby find confidence for our faith. Drawing near to Him in addition to "ascending the tower" are the positions that will ensure this. Thus having understood how to know the word of God, upon knowing it, let us be bold to follow the example of past witnesses in the faith by putting real faith, that is based on God's word, into action.

Principle Two

Faith must be mixed with Righteousness

> *"By faith Abel offered to God a more excellent sacrifice than Cain, through which he obtained witness that he was righteous ... By faith Enoch was taken away so that he did not see death, 'and was not found, because God had taken him'; for before he was taken he had this testimony, that he pleased God."*
>
> Heb 11:4–5

Just as the positioning of the first principle was fitting, the position of this second principle is likewise appropriate. To avoid the misconception that faith can be used like a genie's lamp, which was rubbed whenever its owner needed something, this second principle presents faith as an instrument that is only useable and effective when in the right hands. Faith is a highly effective weapon designed to destroy doubt and to bring God's word to pass. Nevertheless, this will only be the case when faith is complete. In other words, not only must it be marked by unwavering belief and trust in the word of God, but also it must be the essential component which we outlined in the definition earlier: intentional assent to revealed truth such that one yields to the guidance of that truth. This deliberate assent to revealed truth and yielding to its guidance may be summed up in one word, *righteousness*. Without this component, faith is incomplete and actually false. The truth of righteousness being an integral part of faith is evidenced by the remarkable faith demonstrated by each of our ancestors—but it is mentioned explicitly in the examples of Abel and Enoch.

In the familiar story of Cain and Abel we learn that the two brothers offered sacrifices to God (Gen 4:3–4). This is evidently something they must have learned from their parents, Adam and Eve, from a young age. On the only occasion reported of their doing so in Genesis, however, something terrible went wrong. God respected Abel's sacrifice but rejected Cain's. While the details surrounding Cain's sacrifice leading to its rejection are not clearly given, what is clear is either his failure to do something he knew he was supposed to do or his rebelliousness in doing something he was not supposed to do, while carrying out the ritual. In addition, that his actions were sinful was also explicitly stated by God, which was something God also challenged Cain that he should have been aware of (Gen 4:7). Despite all this though, Cain, apparently operating by his own defined "faith," was determined to offer a sacrifice to God, evidently expecting it to atone for his sins, judging from the mere fact of his continuance with the ritual act. He either failed to realize or disregarded the fact that his unrighteousness would negate the benefits of his sacrifice.

As opposed to Cain, Abel demonstrated what God expects of the one who truly has faith in Him. Much is debated over whether God's pleasure in his sacrifice was because it was from *"the firstborn of his flock and of their fat"* (Gen 4:4) as opposed to Cain's, which was of the fruit of the ground, since he was a tiller of the ground (Gen 4:2–3). Keeping in mind that they each brought their gift from their respective labor, however, raises the question of whether this was the reason for God's approval of one and His disapproval of the other.[1] Something else may have been at the root of the issue, but regardless of what that might have been, there's one thing we do know for sure: Abel's actions were characterized as being righteous; meaning he was deliberate to do what was right, while Cain purposed to do what was wrong or unrighteous. In support of this conclusion, we note that the writer of the epistle of First John, in commenting on Cain's motive for murdering Abel, said, *"And why did he murder him? Because his works were evil and his brother's righteous"* (1 John 3:12). Apparently, Abel was keen to observe that God desired more than his ritualistic observances to achieve the benefits of such practices, but interwoven with his ceremonial act was God's requirement that it also be rendered from a righteous life. Even beyond this, not only did Abel do what was right in God's sight, but he also took pleasure in doing so—because God, who knows the heart, must have known this, which led to God's respect of Abel's offering. Righteousness is not just a matter of outward moral conduct to be mechanically performed; but in addition to that, those actions must stem from a heart that is loyal toward God.

---

1. Fretheim, *Pentateuch*, 80; Fretheim, "Genesis," 373.

Now if Abel's actions demonstrated what happens when someone who, by faith, believes God's word and does what His word says to do to achieve a blessing (for Abel offered a sacrifice by faith in the word of God, which he must have heard would atone for his sins in so doing) then the testimony of Enoch takes the reward of mixing righteousness with faith to an even more exciting level. His testimony demonstrates the other side of the spectrum of the remarkable benefits of living righteously where God's favor on our lives to do good for us is concerned. On one side of the spectrum, as seen in the example of Abel, when a righteous person believes God for a promise from His word, the message is that God is eager to grant the desires of that person's heart (Ps 37:4). Now while this is a joy to know, even more joyous is what we see at the other end of the spectrum as illustrated in the example of Enoch: God is eager as well to give to the righteous person even what the individual does not ask for or can imagine!

In the brief account of Enoch's ascent into heaven in Gen 5:18–24, unlike that seen in the case of Elijah where he and the entire school of the prophets were aware beforehand of his heavenly ascent (2 Kgs 2:1–11), there is no mention of Enoch knowing this ahead of time. And even if he did, it is doubtful that he requested it for it probably never came to mind, especially since this was not a usual occurrence; in fact, it was the first ascension in history! Indications then are that God Himself was the originator of the idea, not Enoch, and God chose to do this for Enoch because Enoch walked so closely with God and so pleased Him that God wanted to reward him with something very special for his righteousness, which was to allow him to bypass death by taking him to his eternal home. The testimonies of Abel and Enoch should be encouraging to every person of faith to know that when righteousness is mixed with faith, God is not only willing to demonstrate His favor in granting us our desires that are in agreement with His word, but He is also eager to do exceedingly and abundantly for us, that which we do not even ask for or can imagine (Eph 3:20)!

Being righteous is not a recommendation for enhancing the effectiveness of one's faith, but it is a requirement; righteousness *must* be mixed with faith. This is clear from the testimonies of Abel and Enoch as opposed to Cain's. *It therefore follows that, faith is a tool that is placed in the hands of the righteous, not the unrighteous, to bring into fruition what God promised us in His word.* This point must be underscored because there might be a false notion in the minds of some that it is possible to believe God for something because His word declares it; meanwhile, there is a failure to observe to live in accordance of the same word. One has only to think of the dynamic of a parent-child relationship to understand this. When a parent informs a child that he or she will receive a gift at Christmas, I think even the child who is old enough to understand this and is honest would have to admit that the parent would be sending the wrong message if the parent gives the gift no matter how much that child willfully violates the parent's rules. This is not to say, of course, that the child must be perfect, which, by the way, is a point that will also be explained shortly as it relates to our relationship with God and our expectation to receive anything by faith from Him. Rather, it seems reasonable to expect there to be some conditions for reception implied with not only the promises of a parent, but also God's, unless they are explicitly stated as being without any.

Not only in the dynamic of the parent-child relationship are we able to receive insight into what is reasonable to expect in our relationship with God, but as good an example as any may also be found in the word of God, as seen when the Israelites were about to possess the Promised Land. In Deuteronomy 28, Moses provided a detailed list of many of the promises God made to the nation to give it upon entry: promises of defeat of the enemy, of increase of crop and livestock, of blessings of offspring, among others. Lest the people got the wrong message that these were guaranteed no matter their loyalty or disloyalty to the Lord, however, these blessings were immediately followed by promises of curses if they failed to obey the commandments handed down by Moses. Now of course every promise of blessings in the word of God is not delineated like this where blessings and curses are laid out as our choices based on our obedience to the Lord, yet here is an example where the whole of Scripture must be considered in our understanding of how we receive the promises of God. Because a condition is not attached to a particular promise does not necessarily mean it is not without one, but the student of the word of God should understand the likelihood of there being accompanying conditions with the promise; once again, unless it is stated plainly as being unconditional. So clearly, although God reserves the right to be merciful and to bless us when we are disobedient, God expects us, in addition to believing and trusting Him for His promises, to be obedient to His commandments. Accordingly, righteousness proves to be an integral part of faith.

As we reflect deeper on the relationship between righteousness and faith it should be realized that it is actually natural in many ways that righteousness enhances faith and unrighteousness diminishes and even at times nullifies faith. When we live righteously, we abide in the sphere of God's ability to bless; but when we choose to live otherwise, we place ourselves outside God's blessing. While it should be understood that this is not the exclusive determining factor that decides whether one's faith is effective or not, the fact of it playing a major role in such determination should not be neglected. I think the parable of the "Prodigal Son" makes this point clear (Luke 15:11–32). The younger, beloved son of his father, while at home, had the opportunity to enjoy all the benefits of being his father's child. The period of living at home was the equivalent of living righteously, so to speak, because that time was one of close fellowship with his father and of enjoying all of the joys of being in that fellowship. When he rebelled, however, something tragic happened: the fellowship was broken. The son *himself* had chosen to remove himself from the realm where his father was able to bless him by bestowing on him the benefits of living in his home. Those benefits were automatic with being a resident of the household. This is why when the son came to his senses he realized that the servants in his father's house were better off than him, simply because they lived there. The automatic blessings included shelter, food, and even a sense of belonging. On the other hand, while outside his father's house he lacked even his most basic needs of shelter and food and found it necessary to resort to eating the leftovers of swine. Unrighteousness causes this same catastrophic effect; it robs us of the opportunity to enjoy many of the privileges that being in fellowship with the Lord affords us, even if we say we have faith to believe God for them. Thus, the choice of whether we are going to live in obedience to God's word or not plays a major role in determining what God is able to do for us by faith.

RIGHTEOUSNESS AND PERFECTION

In all likelihood, this discussion of the relationship between righteousness and faith raises some concerns. One possible concern is: to what extent does God expect us to live in obedience to His word for this to be such a determining factor? This is an important and difficult question to answer with precision on behalf of God, which I do not propose to do. Instead, I will put forth a simpler solution to help bring clarity to this issue, which is to make a distinction between righteousness and perfection. By definition, perfection means to be without error of any sort, one hundred percent of the duration of one's entire life, or at least after coming to Christ. But this expectation of any person must be immediately ruled out from this discussion for while it may be argued that the Bible does exhort us to be perfect, it should also be noted that this is not the kind of perfection God expects of us. Rather, Biblical perfection for the people of God is better translated as *maturity*, meaning there should be progress of growth in God as opposed to continual falling into the same sins throughout one's lifetime. Accordingly, what God expects of us when He calls us to righteousness is not perfection but maturity in Him. This is a condition of sustained progression of overcoming sin and vice. On the other hand, the one who is immature willfully continues in sin or is irresponsible in not seeking help and understanding of how to obtain victory over vice and sin through Christ and is thus enslaved to unrighteousness and sin.

Obviously, to suggest that a Christian can be unrighteous is an oxymoron, for how can a person who is clothed in the righteousness of Christ be said to live in unrighteousness (2 Cor 5:21)? To answer this question also requires making yet another distinction—concerning the different works of righteousness performed in us. First, there is righteousness that is immediately bestowed upon us when we give our lives to Christ. This immediate work of righteousness is the kind whereby our status before God is suddenly changed when we come to Him; we are declared to be righteous or justified (Rom 5:1). This is the position of every child of God. The righteousness spoken of in the admonishment to be perfect on the other hand is that which is in practice. This is what the apostle Paul spoke of in Romans 6. In that chapter he urged the saints at Rome to present their entire beings "*as instruments of righteousness to God*" and no longer "*as instruments of unrighteousness to sin*." Apparently, they had become followers of Christ and were declared to be righteous by God, yet in practice they gave themselves over to doing those things which were unrighteous in God's sight. Now the warning issued to them as a result of their behavior is without question also applicable to us as well. As the people of God, we should no longer be enslaved to unrighteousness and sin, but continue to mature in God, giving ourselves over to Him and doing what is pleasing in His sight.

As we have already seen, the ramifications of practicing unrighteousness are severe. When we choose to live in this state, we virtually "tie"

God's hands, even though He longs to do mighty works in and through us. God addressed this same issue with His people through the prophet Isaiah (Isa 59:1–2). God warned them that the reason His power was not revealed among them was not because of His inability, but because of their sins. Now if such was the case then, why should we think the same is not true today? I propose that it is even truer today, because we have the completed canon of Scripture to instruct us in righteousness—something Isaiah's audience did not have; and since *". . . to whom much is given, from him much will be required . . ."* (Luke 12:48), we should be expected to be held to an even greater standard than many of our predecessors. As a result, when we choose to live in sin, even if we think we have unwavering faith in believing God for the promises in His word, we hinder God from doing for us what He desires to do. When we mature in God, however, and continue to grow and strive to please Him continually, the exact opposite happens. In this condition, because faith is now joined with righteousness, when we believe God by faith in His promises, God is not only willing, but also able to honor such faith, because we "untie" His hands. Furthermore, He is now also willing to bless us even beyond our requests, just as He did for Enoch!

The reality of God's intention to do for us beyond what we request or can foresee gives further insight into the amazingly privileged position in which we put ourselves when we live righteously by faith. The mere fact of God's willingness to do such things for us obviously indicates His longing to do them strictly for His own purposes, seeing that we are unaware of what will be done in us. This is supported by the word of the Lord that came to King Asa by Hanani, the seer, in 2 Chr 16:9. God was said to be looking *"throughout the whole earth, to show Himself strong on behalf of those whose heart is loyal to Him."* God was looking for those who practiced righteousness in hopes of doing something awesome in them. Notice, the One who performed the search was God and it was also God who had it in mind to do this awesome thing in those who were faithful to Him, although they were unaware of either the search or the intended action to be performed in and through them. This is what happens when one chooses the path of righteousness! Accordingly, if we understand this, we should require very little additional motivation for living in holiness, knowing that God longs to do great things for and through those who so live!

A CAUTION

Just as this discussion of the rewards of the joining of righteousness and faith in the life of a believer should be exciting to consider, it should, at the same time, also cause some warning lights to go off in our minds. We should be ever mindful of those who, despite their striving to mature in God as God requires, because they do not see the fruit of their faith being realized, draw the conclusion that they must have done something wrong. These include those who have been sick for prolonged periods of time; those who witnessed their loved ones being taken from them despite the offering up of fervent prayers requesting that they remain; those who try all they can and pray believing God to see their economic status improve just enough to make ends meet but do not see it; and so many more. Meanwhile, as these individuals experience this frustration, like "slaps in their faces," they hear others testify of the miracles God performed for them. Furthermore, to make matters worse, they hear what has been suggested thus far concerning the need for righteousness to be joined with faith. If the truth were to be told, many of them know how to mix the two things as well as any other person because they are mostly all they ever had to hold on to! Still, to them the feeling could be one of deep hurt because others dare to suggest that the reason their faith does not "yield" results is because of the presence unrighteousness and sin in their lives.

As we address this difficult problem it is important to keep in mind that receiving from God is dependent on a complexity of factors, and not only whether we believe Him and are living righteously. These may include such things as the need to go through a period of testing at a particular time in order for God to elevate us to another level in Him. Another may be the fact that God has determined in His infinite wisdom that something might not be appropriate for us at a given moment; in other words, God might have all intentions of granting us our wishes but there is a gap between His timing and ours. The issue is thus one that no one should propose to have fully grasped. Understandably though, this clarification might do very little to console many who endeavor to mix righteousness with faith but have not yet experienced some of the benefits that have been indicated to result from such devotedness to God. To them, especially as the pain and intensity persists for a long time, the feeling might be that this is due to some kind of punishment for wrongdoing, or that others perceive it to be the case.

Despite the feeling, however, in reality there is invariably a multiplicity of factors at work, which may not include anything punitive as a consequence of our faults. This being realized, attention must still be paid not to ignore or minimize the importance of the benefits of joining righteousness with faith. We should be persistent in doing so primarily in order to please God, and secondly for reaping the benefits of practicing it. Yet we must not lose sight of the fact that this is a principle that ensures the best outcome of our faith when it is the *only* basis upon which God will determine whether to grant us our longings by faith or not. When God takes other factors into consideration, such as the ones listed above, however, the outcome may not occur the way we hope it will. Whatever the reason, though, we should have confidence in knowing that we can trust God to always have our best interest at heart and to do what is best for us. Simultaneously, we should also understand that there is indication that even when we strive all we can to live holy, God, in His infinite wisdom and for His glory, might still choose to withhold some things from us (see 2 Cor 12:7–10, concerning Paul's thorn in the flesh, for example). Now does this mean that the discussion of righteousness with respect to faith is irrelevant? Taking into account all that has been said so far, absolutely not! First of all, we are called to live holy because God is holy (Lev 19:2), which establishes relevance. By living righteously, we please God; and where faith to believe God is concerned, by living holy we give ourselves the *best* chance possible to achieve results when our faith is added to this kind of living. Then in those cases where other factors are at work, we can have the confidence that God knows what He is doing and will do what is just and best for us.

Now there is at least one other point to consider when exercising care not to send a wrong message to others that suggests they must have done something wrong when such is not the case. Conceivably, many of us may not feel the need to be concerned about this issue since unlike Job's friends who bluntly informed him that he had to have done something wrong to suffer the way he did (Job 4:7–9), we do not usually come close to making such accusations. Indeed, most of us probably would not entertain such line of reasoning when we see another suffer. Nonetheless, in reality we must be aware of this being the way many of those who find themselves in the state of suffering or lack sometimes feel and the messages we send to them, whether intentional or not, can play a major role in contributing to such feelings. The concern, then, is that although we may never send this message deliberately, we should exercise caution not to send it unintentionally either.

One of the areas where there is great risk of unintentionally sending the wrong message is in our testimonies of how faith in God brought about miracles in our lives. In the process of declaring the goodness of God, care must be exercised not to utilize overtones of absolutes, as they actually suggest that the way things happened for us is the manner in which we think faith should always unfold. For example, at times we might testify of believing God for something then having received it, we suggest that our close walk with the Lord in addition to our faith were the sure reasons for obtaining the blessing. Now in light of the above discussion, this possibility must be acknowledged. Yet it must be equally admitted that despite being true on a particular occasion, not every time one walks closely with the Lord will one receive everything one believes God for. We must keep in mind that there are often other factors at work. When we have this awareness, we become careful in our testifying not to give the slightest indication that we intend to suggest that our upright walk before God is the sole reason for receiving the favor of God. On the other hand, while we should not fail to mention the importance of being in close fellowship with the Lord, when we do so, we do it to exhort others to walk likewise. Communicating that this, in conjunction to faith, is the sole reason for our blessings, however, can cause others who have not been bestowed the same blessings due to other reasons to think that God is punishing them for some wrongdoing, although God might be well pleased with their walk.

And what about bragging about how strong our faith is and how we "never" wavered when we set out to believe God? Again, this may be true and it is commendable when it is the case. Yet as essential as unwavering belief is, sometimes that alone is not the only determining factor as to whether we receive the things for which we trust in God. Moreover, as a result, there may be others who believe just like we do but do not see the results they desire. So while testifying of unwavering faith is good, there should be a balance in our testimonies to consider leaving room for other variables that may be at work in the process of receiving the blessing, since unwavering belief is not the only determining factor in the process. Now I do not intend in any way to discourage testifying of one's faith; on the contrary, I encourage it. This is what Hebrews 11 is all about because it provides testimonies of the faith of others in order to inspire faith in us. Nevertheless, just as that chapter is balanced in incorporating a wide range of principles about faith, so should our testimonies, in like manner, be balanced.

The importance of heeding this caution is vital because of the potential not only for us to cause others' hopes to be destroyed, but to also cause them to question their faith as a whole. Just maybe the severity of the potential risk at hand can be imagined if for a moment we picture ourselves as the ones being faced with a life threatening illness, an eviction notice, or any similarly devastating news; meanwhile, the message perceived to come from others is that we do not believe enough or we did something wrong, although we know how much we believe and how much we shun evil. Such perception can be destructive to faith, especially when we are in such a vulnerable state. On the other hand, with correct teaching and testimonies that do justice to what the Lord has truly done, even when in such vulnerable states, most, even if not at first, should be encouraged to rejoice with others who have already experienced their victory. Remember, if for no other reason, we must keep in mind that we all have the responsibility of being our brothers' and sisters' care-givers, so we must be concerned enough about their lives and faith to be careful not to place stumbling blocks in their paths (Rom 14:13; 1 Cor 8:9).

RIGHTEOUSNESS THROUGH FAITH

In the overall discussion of the need for righteousness to be joined with faith there is an important concept that must not be misunderstood. Herein is one of those instances where one should be able to see a glimpse into the wisdom of the Holy Spirit in putting together the word of God. In Heb 11:4–5, we see the examples of how faith worked in both Abel and Enoch because of their upright walk before God. But just so we do not get the wrong message that this upright walk was the result of some inner good in those individuals nor think to say the same of ourselves, in the following verse (v. 6) the reader is suddenly reminded of the true source of that righteousness; it was through faith. In that verse, faith is not presented as a possible means to consider whereby one can live to please God (pleasing God being synonymous with righteousness), but as being essential to the process for without it, pleasing God becomes a virtual impossibility! So while it is true that righteousness is necessary for faith, even more importantly, faith is first necessary for righteousness to be possible. It was by faith, therefore, that both Abel and Enoch were able to achieve the testimony of being righteous, and it is by faith that we are able to obtain it as well. In truth, then, in the discussion of the need for righteousness to be mixed with faith, the concept is complex, for we actually become righteous by faith. Righteousness, in turn, comes into play to work with our faith, causing us to receive the things we do by faith; thus the two are inseparable where real faith is concerned.

Whether we are aware of it or not, there is the potential in us to think we can live righteously in our own strength based on our ability to withstand some temptations. This is perhaps most likely to happen when there are known temptations that come our way but which clearly seem to have no influence over us. The ensuing deception is to reflect on those victories and use them as motivation to believe we can withstand the temptation of other things that we do have an appetite for and to whose "power" we therefore are susceptible. Then soon the reality sets in: we find ourselves falling continually into sin in those areas. This can be frustrating and deflating, and the only escape is to acknowledge that no matter the temptation we face, to consider overcoming such temptation in our own strength is simply an act of futility. The practice, by the way, of weighing our own strength against a temptation, is the ultimate source, not only of our failure, but also of our frustration. In using this approach, we sometimes find it possible to enjoy victory over some temptations; but in reality we may not have had an appetite for them in the first place. That approach to temptation is a trap, and when we fall into it we will ultimately fail, leading to unrighteousness and sin; and for the one who desires to be righteous, this can be frustrating.

To avoid this, we must utilize the only means that God has provided to enable us to please Him—faith. To rely on faith means to trust God for the strength to withstand every temptation. God will provide it and will also instruct us how to escape future temptations (see 1 Cor 10:13). Everything that has to do with our dealings with God must be by faith. This begins with first believing that He is or exists, Hebrews 11:6 continues, which is inferred as only being possible by faith since no one has ever seen God. Now if the knowledge of God can only come by faith, how much more the ability to please Him? Evidently it can only come by faith as well. Once this is understood and embraced, it becomes a joy instead of a frustration to know that righteousness must be joined with faith, because we then cease to strive to obtain righteousness in our own strength—but only in that which God supplies by faith. Of course temptations will still come because the devil, having already lost everything, has nothing more to lose, so he keeps trying. This is why we find that sometimes there may be periods when a temptation is no longer placed before us, or if it is, we can turn our backs on it with relative "ease" as compared to other times. It is during the hard times however that the devil keeps coming back. Remember, he did the same with Christ in leaving Him until an "*opportune time*" (Luke 4:13). He did this because it is his strategy, although in the case of Christ there was no true "*opportune time*," since Christ defeated him every time. But in our case, if we do not rely on God's strength by faith every time, we will find numerous periods in our lives when the devil can truly say he caught us at an "*opportune time.*" The victory is ours, however, if we, by faith alone, endeavor to please God.

There is yet another exciting way in which the truth that righteousness must be joined with faith should be a great source of comfort and encouragement. The ending of Hebrews 11:6 assures us that God *"is a rewarder of those who diligently seek Him."* When we consider the price that must be paid, and it is indeed a price to live godly lives, we sometimes can become frustrated in losing sight of the rewards for doing so. If we lose focus and concentrate instead on gratifying the flesh, the sentiment can easily become: "What's the use, what profit is there in remaining pure and to burn with passion when I can enjoy sexual relations now"? Or, "Why should I be honest when the dishonest seem to enjoy life"? Or, "Does anyone even notice, or care"? Such questions we begin to ask within ourselves when we lose sight of the prize, leading to the possible conclusion that the way of righteousness is too hard and not worth the trouble.

But be comforted and encouraged, says the writer, God is faithful and just, and God will reward us fairly for every effort put forth to please Him! This truth is affirmed and confirmed throughout the word of God and often even in our own experiences, which should give us confidence that even when we do not yet see the benefits or the rewards, God will still come through in being faithful to keep His promises (1 Cor 15:58; Heb 6:10). This is an amazing concept in that what sometimes appears to be a pain and to no avail ultimately turns out to be for our own good since we will receive a reward! The simple fact that we please God should be sufficient motivation to holiness, being our reasonable service to Him, since it was for this purpose we were created (see Rom 12:1). In His great love, favor, and grace, however, the Lord sees fit to prepare prizes for us for doing so, and not just for eternity, but also for this life. So while it is true that living godly comes with a price (Luke 14:27–33), the cost is nothing to be compared to the rewards that are sure to follow (Rom 8:18).

Above all, the benefits of living a godly life are infinitely better than the alternative. Let me be clear, there is absolutely no benefit, even in the present, to living in ungodly ways. The truth is: what might appear to be beneficial in committing sin is really only a trick of the enemy of our souls. Once more, there is absolutely no benefit in unrighteousness! When we see only through our natural eyes and not through the eyes of faith instead, we are likely to conclude the exact opposite and end up sinning, thinking there is some advantage. The Bible makes it clear, however, "... *the way of the unfaithful is hard*" (Prov 13:15b). Furthermore, this hardship should not be taken as only occurring in the afterlife, but also in the present. The comparison is therefore not even a comparison at all: there is absolutely no benefit in unrighteousness; it is impossible to compare it to the rewards of righteousness, which are infinite when considered both for this life and for the one to come.

The verdict is unanimous: righteousness must not only be mixed with faith, but to think or live otherwise would be to deprive oneself of his or her own blessings! In light of the amazing benefits which we understand to be ours, we should be energized and motivated to live godly lives! It is clear that God is longing to reward us for our faith, even in ways that are beyond the realm of what we have faith to imagine. Accordingly, the charge to join righteousness with faith as Abel and Enoch did should not be received with regret, but with exceeding joy.

Principle Three

Faith requires doing the "Ridiculous"

"By faith Noah, being divinely warned of things not yet seen, moved with godly fear, prepared an ark for the saving of his household, by which he condemned the world and became heir of the righteousness which is according to faith. By faith Abraham obeyed when he was called to go out to the place which he would receive as an inheritance. And he went out, not knowing where he was going. By faith he dwelt in the land of promise as in a foreign country, dwelling in tents with Isaac and Jacob, the heirs with him of the same promise; for he waited for the city which has foundations, whose builder and maker is God."

Heb 11:7–10

"By faith the walls of Jericho fell down after they were encircled for seven days."

Heb 11:30

"By faith Joseph, when he was dying, made mention of the departure of the children of Israel, and gave instructions concerning his bones."

Heb 11:22

These four testimonies of faith by the elders, Noah, Abraham, Joseph, and Joshua who led the Hebrew people at Jericho, introduces the third principle of faith in emphatic and dramatic fashion. This principle, as we shall see, is integral to every action of faith; it is *always* present. If the testimonies of each of the witnesses were to be studied carefully, it should be discovered that they all displayed this tenacity. They all demonstrated some measure of "ridiculousness" in their faith—some to a greater extent than others, but perhaps none more so than Noah, Abraham, Joseph, and Joshua. Beginning with Noah, by condensing the story into just one verse, the writer obviously assumes the reader's familiarity with the story to appreciate just how amazing this man's faith was. Still, he conveys a glimpse into it by the use of such skillfully crafted phrases as, "*being divinely warned of things not yet seen,*" and Noah being "*moved with godly fear,*" then caps it all off with the action of Noah that we can say characterized his faith as "ridiculous." But before elaborating on his actions, there is a possible dispute that I think should be dealt with upfront. Some might argue that Noah simply acted out of fright since the Scripture states that he was "*moved with godly fear.*" Such a claim is easily refuted however by noting that Noah's godly fear, like the godly fear Abraham and many others in Scripture had, is not to be understood so much as referring to fright but to awe resulting in obedience.[1] Furthermore, fright alone does not guarantee sustained loyalty and obedience over time when the judgment being forewarned about is delayed. In fact, one might argue that it virtually never does, yet Noah sustained his reverent fear long enough to build a large ship using primitive tools.

So Noah built the ark in a place where there was apparently no water in sight sufficient to sail such a vessel as he prepared for a flood that would destroy all flesh on earth, except marine life. Imagine what it must have looked like to the people in the area to see him and his family do this, and the jeering that no doubt ensued! How foolish it must have appeared to see the animals boarding the ark. To us today this story is inspiring both spiritually and artistically as there are so many depictions of this story in art. But can it be said that Noah's generation had this same level of appreciation for these things? I think we can safely say they did not for there was not as much as one believer outside his family that entered the ark, indicating that what he did must have seemed foolish to onlookers. But this is precisely what made his faith "ridiculous." When everyone else questioned his actions in disbelief and considered them to be foolish, Noah persisted in obedience to the word of God, even though it may have contradicted his own reasoning. In addition, although the Genesis account does not mention any threat of dissension by his family, it is conceivable that it was present nonetheless. The word of the Lord came directly to Noah and his family was left to decide whether or not they

---

1. Mann, *Torah*, 47.

would support him, which they evidently did. Still, they may have only done so in obedience to him as the patriarch of the family, although likely with complaining, questioning, and even doubting. No wonder the writer of Hebrews spoke only of Noah's faith although there were seven others that were with him in the ark; for he was, as it were, standing all alone in obedience to the "outrageous" demands of his faith.

And what about the actions of our father Abraham who uprooted his family from its "stable" foundations in Ur of the Chaldeans, to go to a land that he had never seen or visited but the reality of which was only to be found in the promise of God? Today most of us, if we are careful, would only migrate if the conditions in our present home are no longer desirable and we are certain that those in our potentially new home will be more favorable. We make the move only if we have seen pictures or made a prior visit, we have heard testimonies of others who have made a similar move, we believe we will be welcomed by those who already live there, and we have investigated and concluded that the opportunities there would be ones available to us. Conversely, we are not told of Abraham having any such information to influence his actions; rather, he seemed to have been established in his original home as a wealthy and no doubt respected individual. He possessed everything by which wealth was measured in his day—servants, livestock, silver and gold (Gen 13:2, 6). Evidently he already had everything he needed and desired in order to live a luxurious life in Ur of the Chaldeans. Nevertheless, he was willing to uproot his foundations and live as a nomad, dwelling in tents, in obedience of the word of God to get out of his country in order to inherit a *"city which has foundations, whose builder and maker is God"* (Heb 11:10). This display of obedience and trust in the word of God is thus another example of "absurdity"!

The scene of the children of Israel marching around the walls of Jericho once per day for six days then seven times on the seventh day is likewise extraordinary. If there is ever a discussion of what the most "ridiculous" actions of all the acts of faith are, not only in Hebrews 11, but in all of Scripture, and this one was excluded, such exclusion would be a sign of a lack of familiarity with the story. In ancient times a walled city was a well fortified one, especially if it had everything it needed within its walls to make it self-sufficient. Jericho was one such city, and the Israelites knew it. Even if it did not have a strong army, by the mere fact that it could not be penetrated made it a well protected city since there was no other way to threaten it than to scale its walls or to break down its impenetrable gates. Despite the reports of what the children of Israel had done to other nations beyond the Jordan no doubt the people of Jericho felt secure within their walled city. We can only imagine what went through their minds as they looked over the walls and saw the Israelites encircling their mighty fortress. While the Israelites may have appeared to be a mighty army, the strategy they employed to overcome the barrier of the walls by encircling them for days must have seemed foolish. No one had ever heard of walls falling down after being encircled, but that was about to change! The seemingly absurd action was precisely what God had purposed for the Israelites to obtain the victory over the otherwise undefeatable city. It was thus only by faith in the word of God that the people, led by Joshua, were able to accomplish this feat. They not only believed the promise of God that they would obtain the victory, but were willing to demonstrate that belief by doing the "ridiculous"!

Finally, the faith of Joseph perhaps tops the charts of doing the "ridiculous." To build an ark in the middle of nowhere as Noah did was "ridiculous"; to leave a life of comfort and stability for another that was only a promise as Abraham did was also "ridiculous"; and to march around the walls of Jericho as Joshua and his followers did in order to bring them down was likewise "ridiculous." But what Joseph did appears to have topped them all on the "ridiculous" chart. Interestingly, what Noah, Abraham, and Joshua did depended on them. Although they received help, this was still the case because they had the influence necessary to procure the assistance they needed from others such as family in the case of Noah, family and servants in the case of Abraham, and the entire nation in the case of Joshua. Furthermore, they were present throughout the effort to carry out and to supervise up to completion what they set out to accomplish by faith. In comparison, Joseph, in giving instructions concerning his bones that they should not remain in Egypt forever but be carried up to the land of promise, had no way of carrying this out himself or supervising it—but depended on the faithfulness and obedience of others to this command, and that over 400 years later!

In considering the faith of Joseph we may say it was one thing to make mention of the departure of the children of Israel while he was dying, as that was not unusual for the patriarchs to speak of things to come and to pronounce blessings before dying (see, for example, Gen 27, 48 & 49). Even the mention of the burial of his bones was not unusual to an extent, because Jacob had caused Joseph himself to swear he would not bury him in Egypt (Gen 47:29–31). What was unusual however was the timeframe in which Joseph's bones were expected to be carried to their final resting place on earth. Unlike Jacob who could depend on his own son, a prominent figure in Egypt, to take his body up out of Egypt to be buried in the land of promise, Joseph depended on others in future generations for whom he would cease to be of personal—but only historical—influence to uphold the oath. The many variables that could jeopardize the wish such as neglect, unfaithfulness, and time itself, are clear. Yet, against these odds and others, Joseph took the oath by faith, believing that his bones would be carried up to the land of promise along with the children of Israel. He hoped against these variables and expected the people to honor his request despite the fact of the possibility of their considering his remains to be nothing of value to them such as silver and gold, just the bones of someone who would have died centuries earlier. Again, in addition to that, because he was not able to see and monitor that it would be carried out faithfully, his testimony of faith was perhaps the most "ridiculous" of all.

"RIDICULOUSNESS" IS INHERENT IN FAITH

I think it is now clear from the display of faith by the witnesses, Noah, Abraham, Joshua, and Joseph, that doing the "ridiculous" is integral to the walk of faith. This is simply an undeniable aspect of faith. The simple proof of this assertion is in the reality that what faith promises is always something not yet seen and unobtainable by natural means; otherwise, there would be no need for faith since we would have the ability to do the same in our own strength. This being the case, faith is guaranteed to be doubted by at least one person, and often by the majority of onlookers, even occasionally by everyone else besides the person who believes! This guarantee is what causes faith always to seem ridiculous. The classification of being "ridiculous" is thus "fitting" for faith simply because it is a constant in every occurrence of faith: it will seem absurd to doubters.

Indeed God tends to specialize in doing that which absolutely goes against the grain. God always seems to use methods that are contrary to conventional wisdom. Consequently, His ways always appear to be outrageous to the one who only sees with natural eyes. Just when one's mental capacity has been exhausted and all possibilities of seeing a way out of difficulty prove futile, God speaks a word that things will work out in unimaginable ways. Then, because God's methods are not conventional, the naturally-minded, unable to accept the divine plan, doubt and regard anyone else who chooses to believe as being ones who trust in something absurd. The folly of such resolve is to forget that God's ways are not our ways, or humans would be equal to God. His ways transcends ours, which is why, as Paul declared, His ways are *"past finding out"* (Rom 11:33). Nevertheless, many simply refuse to accept this, and to their own demise, fail to trust God for the good outcome.

Unfortunately, although we should know better, because many of us who believe detect this tendency in the majority of those we know, we repeatedly allow ourselves to be robbed of the blessings that are in store for us by faith because we are overly concerned about the opinions of others. There is a remarkable weakness in humans as a whole in that we can know with assurance what is best for us yet allow the influence and opinions of others to veer us off the path to wellbeing. Sadly, while the people of God should be able to rise above this weakness, since we know the blessings of trusting in God by faith, we frequently allow ourselves to fall prey to the same weakness. But herein is another aspect of the "ridiculousness" which we must demonstrate in our faith: to resolve to stand fast with confidence in what we believe in the face of opposition and ridicule, just as the elders evidently did.

Notice to this point I have put the word "ridiculous," as well as other words having the same connotation, in quotations because obviously the "ridiculousness" of faith is only a reality to the one who fails to trust in the word of God by faith. In reality, there is absolutely nothing ridiculous about the word which God speaks—written or unwritten—concerning anything! Because it is His word and He has all power and authority to bring it to fruition, it can be counted on! As a result, then, what is ridiculous is a person's failure to believe the word which the almighty God of the universe and beyond has declared! For how can we but believe Him? This is why Jesus, when He walked this earth, occasionally marveled at the lack of faith of many in His day (see, for example, Mark 6:6). It should be sufficient for us to trust Him simply because He is God; yet in His generosity, He has made His track record available to us, which is open for investigation, to encourage us to trust Him. Upon investigating it, anyone should find convincing evidence that God always honors His word and has never allowed even one tittle, the smallest stroke in a Hebrew letter, to fail (Matt 5:18)! Not to trust in His word therefore is what is amazingly ridiculous.

MATURITY AND FAITH

Key to comprehending the "ridiculous" nature of faith is being aware of the influence of an important variable, which plays a major role in determining the level of "absurdity" that *will* be demanded of our faith. That variable is our level of maturity in our walk with God. As a reminder, every step of faith we take will include some measure of "foolishness" because it is inherent in faith, and the extent of the measure of "foolishness" involved will depend on how mature one is in God. Now it is one thing that everything God calls us to do by faith will be considered by many to be absurd; but some things just do not fit on the scale of absurdity, they go off the charts! They do not only make us look like we're doing something insane but that we ourselves have gone insane! Often we are caused to stop in amazement and to ponder what God has asked, wondering if God Himself has made a mistake, though we know that's not possible; but so taken aback, we become irrational momentarily. Should we look back over the course of our duration of walking with the Lord, I think we will find that these incidents of "over the top" demands of our faith actually increase in intensity with longevity of fellowship with the Lord. The reason for this is because as we grow in maturity in God, He takes us to greater levels of faith in Him.

As we reflect on this process I think it is important for us to understand that, despite how burdened we might feel from time to time, due to the intense nature of what will be demanded of us as we take this journey of faith, this path is by no means one that the Lord takes us on simply because He has the ability to do so or because He takes pleasure in putting us under stress. On the contrary, there are actually greater purposes at work in the process that make this journey both necessary and indeed a joy to undergo. First, it is a route that takes the mature from one level of maturity to other levels of maturity. What else should be expected to happen if someone steps out by faith in the word of God to do something extraordinary and sees God come through, than for that person to learn to trust God for the next thing that is even more extraordinary? Logically, this would seem to be the path of progressive faith growth, and when things unfold this way, a person's faith grows, and his/her level of maturity likewise increases in the process. God thus takes us on strategic pathways in our journey of faith to help us grow in Him; but those pathways must increase from one level of "foolishness" to greater levels of "foolishness" in order for us to attain to the full stature that God has ordained for us to accomplish in Him.

This is why I pointed out earlier that if we should look back over the course of our walk with the Lord we should notice the level of "absurdity" in our faith increasing with time as we progressed in Him. This is one of the many means the Lord uses to grow us and to develop our spiritual digestive systems so that they do not forever remain incapable of digesting strong meat and only capable of digesting milk. If this process does not exemplify our faith experience, then I propose that something is drastically wrong and in need of immediate attention. It suggests stagnation or, even worse, regression; certainly it is a lack of growth, which is highly problematic! If the problem is learning to trust God, which allows Him to increase the demands on our faith in order for us to grow thereby, then we must give attention to do so. If, on the other hand, our lack of maturity is due to a love for unrighteousness more than righteousness, then we must repent and trust God to grow us in holiness.

Another reason why God takes us on the journey of increased "ridiculousness" in our faith is because this demand comes naturally with what He calls the mature to do; meanwhile, such a demand cannot be entrusted to the immature. Just as "ridiculousness" is inherent in faith, so are increased levels of "ridiculousness" inherent in the tasks given to those who are taken from one level of maturity to another. When we are babes in Christ, "baby" demands will be placed on our faith; but as we grow in Him, He calls us to perform those roles for the kingdom that only the "seasoned" can accomplish because they will require the employment of faith of the most "ridiculous" sort. As we complete one task, God places even further demands on our faith as He calls us to something greater, which automatically requires an increased demand of "foolishness" of our faith. Accordingly, when we understand this process, there should be a joy in knowing that there are greater levels of maturity awaiting us as we take the journey. Also of equal excitement should be the realization that God intends to do great things both in and through us. Furthermore, as we continue to develop in Him, we should be confident in knowing we will most surely share in the accomplishments of exploits for the kingdom. Thus, maturity and doing the "ridiculous" go hand in hand in faith; and when this dynamic is fully understood, it becomes a joy for the righteous to consider being a part of it.

The notion of "ridiculousness" as being a part of faith must not be misunderstood as being justification for anyone to engage in acts of hatred or violence against another person or against society in the name of God. Such behavior is alien to the present discussion. In Colossians 3:12–17, the apostle Paul gave a succinct description of the character of the regenerated person. Key traits listed are being merciful, kind, humble, meek, being patient with one another, and forgiving. Above all, the apostle exhorted, that person must be a loving person, because love "*is the bond of perfection*" (Col 3:14). Having the desire to inflict harm against another, therefore, is contradictory to the character of the person who is truly of faith in Christ. Any act of hatred or violence must be ruled out of the discussion of what a "ridiculous" act of faith is; instead, it must be acknowledged as being sinful! On the contrary, while faith does require that we perform "ridiculous" acts, those prescribed acts will not contradict the love of Christ, which abides in the regenerate, and from which he/she should operate.

"FAITH RADICALS"

Considering all that has been said thus far regarding the intrinsic "ridiculousness" that is in faith as well as its increased measure of intensity in one's faith with growth in God, I think it would be appropriate to consider those who take this walk of faith as "Faith Radicals"—"radical" because we are courageous in not only believing God for the impossible, but we are bold enough to do the necessary works even before we see fulfillment, much like Abraham did in stepping out by faith before seeing the Promised Land. Yet we are not radical in our own strength, confidence, or definition, but by faith alone in the word of God. As should be noted when reading each account of the heroes of faith in Hebrews 11, each individual can be said to have been a "Faith Radical" because they were all courageous in accomplishing feats that required stepping out on faith to do what was far-reaching and beyond human comprehension. And now what is amazing and should also be of great comfort is the knowledge and understanding that the designation was not reserved for them only. God Himself reserved it in advance for all those who would, as they did, believe Him for everything He promised.

This truth emphasizes the importance of understanding our responsibility to know just what has been prepared for us. In this respect, Ephesians 2:10 was not only applicable for those at Ephesus, but also for us today: *"For we are His workmanship, created in Christ Jesus for good works, which God prepared beforehand that we should walk in them."* From this passage it is clear that God has carved out some works as gifts for His children to fulfill; but before we can even begin to walk in them, we must first know what they are. One of those works, I am convinced, is that we ultimately become "Faith Radicals." In truth, all of God's children are "Faith Radicals" whether or not we realize it; although in light of what we have seen thus far from the witnesses in the faith as compared to many of us, evidently some are more so than others, but all of us are "Faith Radicals" nonetheless. We became that way the moment we received Christ as Lord and Savior, which is the first and most radical step of all.

Yes, as radical as building an ark was; or leaving the comfort of one's place of origin in search of another of promise; or giving instructions about one's bones to be carried out by a future generation centuries removed from one's death; or any other act of faith was and is—none is as radical as turning around one's direction in life 180 degrees to follow someone else, namely, Christ, whom we have not seen, but believe in! Anyone who has done this is actually a "Faith Radical." This is indeed the first and most essential of the good works that the apostle Paul wrote of, which God has prepared for us to walk in. Until we walk in this essential good work, all other good works that have been prepared are not options for us, which is a truth that is supported by the second principle of faith: *faith must be mixed with righteousness.* Since believing in Christ is the most essential good work among all the radical ones that God has foreordained for us, then literally by definition it has also become the chief radical act of faith that anyone can possibly engage in. This being the case, every child of God also by definition is a "Faith Radical." Sadly, though, what is of great concern is that most of us either do not realize this; or, despite realizing it, continue to walk as if we do not, by failing to step out in faith to do the "ridiculous."

But having taken this first and most important step of faith, there is absolutely no reason why we should not be motivated to take all others that are only fitting and expected for "Faith Radicals" to take. We must view them simply as good works, which the Father prepared beforehand for us to walk in. Now we might think to say we lack the capacity to believe God.

But how is it that we can believe in God for the most difficult one—believing that He exists, which is the most difficult truth about God to believe according to Hebrews 11:6—yet doubt Him for other promises that find their basis in this first and fundamental truth? Or if the opinion of others has become the stumbling block to our success in stepping out in faith on the word of God to affirm our positions in God as "Faith Radicals," why are we so concerned about their opinions now, seeing we have already ignored it where the most "foolish" thing about faith in God is concerned, which is salvation through the cross of Christ (1 Cor 1:18–29)? We must embrace the reality of our being radical in faith, indeed to the greatest extent, because we believe in Christ as Savior, and thereby be motivated to believe and walk in any promise of God, no matter how "ridiculous."

Upon embarking on the journey of becoming "Faith Radicals," I consider all other good works that have been prepared for us to walk in by faith, and which the world characterizes as being "ridiculous," as being under two categories: ministry and individual wellbeing. Although these two are actually inseparable because they go hand in hand and depend on each other, I will treat them separately for the purpose of discussion. In order for God to be glorified in these two areas, it is mandatory that we walk consistently as "Faith Radicals" and do the "absurd" by faith. There is simply no alternative to this process. Furthermore, as a reminder, the farther along we are in the journey, the more radical we must become, and the more "absurd" the things we will be called to do will seem.

FAITH RADICALS IN MINISTRY

In the first category—ministry—to illustrate the increase in the level of demand to do what is radical that comes with maturity, I will use myself as an example, having been on a faith journey for several years now, which has resulted in my present calling as Pastor. Just over twenty years ago, I became a "Faith Radical" by accepting Jesus as my Lord and Savior. For the next sixteen years I took many steps by faith and did what may have seemed foolish in the sight of the world. This included the giving of large portions of my earnings to the work of God, volunteering much of my personal time to do service in the ministry without seeking any financial or other personal gain, investing much of my own money and time to study in Bible School and Seminary while working a full-time job without any particular goal in mind or hopes of receiving anything in return, and numerous other acts of faith, which the naturally-minded person might never appreciate.

Then, haven proven me to be trustworthy to do the things I just mentioned, the Lord saw fit to call me to another level of radicalism in my faith. This required not only that I enter the pastorate, but that I should move from New York City—the place where I had lived for almost eighteen years and had come to know many people, who I am confident would have joined me in the work—to Conyers, Georgia, a city that I had never heard of, to start the ministry immediately upon arrival without having the assurance of anyone else joining the church beside my wife and our infant daughter. Having been in the work for just over three years now, the story of the call to "ridiculous" faith has not ended; rather, in keeping with the process, it has intensified. We have been called to step out on faith to purchase land, which we have done, and to prepare to build a church before seeing the personnel that one might expect would be necessary to accomplish this feat by human standards. In stepping out on faith, however, God has accomplished through us that which defies the estimation of many concerning what should have been necessary to do so; and the best yet to come.

Make no mistakes about it, my tour of faith is by no means unique, but similar faith is chronicled in the lives of many who have gone on before me and many who are doing the same and far more today. It will also continue to be the testimony of many to come, just as it is ours today and was for many who were before us. With ministry comes the requirement of doing things that are neither completely understood nor figured out. Anyone who has ever been or is presently involved in ministry can testify to this. Ministry is essentially a call to radicalism in one's faith. It requires stepping out to do things for the Lord in defiance of not only conventional wisdom, but also of common sense at times, by the world's standards. Unfortunately, many in ministry still have not come to grips with this truth, leading to incomplete and ineffective missions for God. Often we commenced a journey to do what God commissioned us to do; but somewhere along the road when we were called to a greater level of trust, we doubted, which led to not only a pause, but a halt in the work, as we abandoned the journey only shortly after beginning.

Just like deeply impressed footprints left behind by an escaped convict on a muddy trail, which does not require a blood hound to track, many of us have engraved our footprints in numerous ministry efforts, but have left them unfinished. The footprints are distinctly ours, and everyone knows it. Now we must ask ourselves what happened, why we did not finish the task. As we reflect on these things, I propose that if we are honest, we would admit that in those cases when we were certain of God's commissioning but we still failed to continue in the work, our failure was strictly a result of a lack of trust in God to accomplish the hard thing in us. That hard thing may have been to spend a bit more money than we were comfortable "giving up"; or quitting a job and trusting God to supply all our need; or leaving our country and our kindred to go to another where many uncertainties awaited us; or stepping out on faith to start a ministry when all the finances were not yet in order; or a whole host of other situations that required doing something radical, but we just were not "ridiculous" enough in our faith to believe God to bring them to pass.

If we expect to advance in ministry as God would have us to do, as opposed to remaining at our beginning stage, then the above scenario must change. Referring to the assertion of the first principle—faith must be based on the word of God—once we are certain we have heard from God, we must be courageous in our belief in God and trust Him to take us from one level in ministry to another and stop doubting Him, no matter how "absurd" the task may be. We simply must learn to *"walk by faith, not by sight"* (2 Cor 5:7). We must cease to allow the kingdom to suffer want, because of our fears and concerns of the opinions of others. God has chosen to limit Himself in many ways by commissioning us to accomplish His work. This is in part what Jesus spoke of when He said the harvest was plentiful but the laborers were few (Matt 9:37). Not only are there too few laborers to begin with; but of the few that God has, some put their hands to the plough, and for some reason, one of which is a lack of faith to trust Him fully in the call, leave the work incomplete. When this happens, the number of available laborers in the field, already few, is further diminished, thus causing much of the harvest to rot. This tendency must be abated if the kingdom is to advance. God is counting on us! Let us therefore show ourselves as true "Faith Radicals" and perform what we have been called to do.

FAITH RADICALS IN INDIVIDUAL WELLBEING

As was mentioned above, ministry and individual or personal wellbeing go hand in hand; the two are inseparable. I do realize that this assertion might be a revolutionary idea to some since the tendency of late seems to be to view the two as being separate and distinct. Scripture does reveal God's intentions to bless each person in immeasurable ways (e.g., Ps 40:5). Indeed, God has privileged us in outlining many of these blessings in the pages of Scripture for us to claim. It is thus our right to know them and to trust God for them. This is an example where our familiarity with what Scripture declares about us and being confident in knowing when God has spoken a word into our spirits, proves vital. Once God has spoken a word to us, we should have the confidence of knowing we can believe Him for those promises to come to fruition. This is also a point where "ridiculous" faith must be put into action. Remember, in all likelihood, most will not believe the word that God speaks to us. It will seem foolish, and there might even be scientific evidence to contradict it, such as against a promise of healing because all indications suggest the imminence of death. Similar indications of loss, not to life but to a circumstance, may also be encountered, such as a foreclosure notice issued by the bank, or divorce papers signifying the end of a marriage. If God speaks a word to the contrary however, it must take precedence in our hearts over these reports and believed on with all our might! This must be the resolve of a "Faith Radical."

It is thus our right to believe God and His promises. But despite this right, it appears there is much wisdom in evaluating the worth of even these promises of personal blessings by how they can help in ministry; and there are good reasons to support doing so. First, it appears we actually walk a very fine line where our desires and yearnings are concerned. Because of them we risk falling on the side of pursuing selfish ambitions—one of the lusts of the flesh (Gal 5:20). In desiring personal blessings, we must therefore be careful to have the end result in mind after receiving them. For example, could it be that we long to boast and flaunt the awesome blessings that God has bestowed upon us before others; or to so enjoy them that we no longer have time for the work of the One who blessed us with them; or to have some other lustful or prideful purpose in mind? Because of the second possibility in particular, I am convinced that our individual wellbeing and ministry were intended to go hand in hand. As we put our desires before the Lord, it would be wise to confess to God from the heart how we intend to use the blessings for His glory, which is ministry. This can help safeguard against selfish ambitions. Do we seek a financial blessing to also help bless God's work in the process, or do we intend to graduate to another level in our robbery of the portion belonging to God—the tithe—by doing so from a larger amount; or even if we will give this portion to God, will we allow the rest to cause us to diminish our time and devotion to Him? Similarly, I think it will be good to tell the Lord how we intend to use even our healing for His glory. If it is simply to testify, and certainly not to boast, to others or to take the opportunity to use it as a point of encouragement to others who are sick, that is ministry. On the other hand, if we desire it so that we can continue to pursue our personal goals and pleasures only, then we are selfish, and God has become for us only a means to accomplish that end. So because we walk such a fine line, it is wise to evaluate our desired blessings in terms of how we intend to use them to bring glory to God, which, again, is ministry.

Along this line, I think it is safe to say that Jesus' admonishment, that we "*seek first the kingdom of God and His righteousness*" (Matt 6: 33), trusting that all the things we long for will be added to us, validates what I have proposed. Love for God and doing His will must come first in the desires of our hearts, and then every other desire should flow out of this longing to please Him. Excitingly, coming from a heart like this, the Lord is pleased to grant us our petitions that conform to with His will (Ps 37:4). Accordingly, there is absolutely no loss in putting the work of God first, only gain! Number one, it helps to safeguard against selfishness; and secondly, it also guarantees that God will be pleased, and if we remember the example of Enoch, when God is pleased, God takes pleasure in doing unimaginable things for us.

Now the other reason why it is wise to evaluate the significance of personal blessings only in terms of their worth for ministry should require very little convincing of the reason. How should it look to the One who blesses us if we do not intend to bless Him in return with that with which He has blessed us? It will not be good; in fact, I believe it will be hurtful even to God! In support of this strong conclusion, I ask this question of the reader: how do you think Jesus felt when He healed the ten lepers but only one returned to give God the glory (Luke 17:11–19)? I think He was saddened. This seems to be the clear indication from the story as He was noted as emphasizing the fact that the only one who returned was a foreigner, which implied that the other nine were His fellow countrymen who were expected to show the greater gratitude. How hurtful? I believe Jesus, being God in the flesh, showed us a side of God, to which we need to pay close attention. God is saddened when we take His blessings and consume them upon our lusts while neglecting His need, which is to advance the kingdom.

So yes it is our right and our privilege to be radical in our faith to believe God for every promised blessing. We should familiarize ourselves with them and lay hold on them because it is God's good pleasure to give them to us. We must be certain that the word which we claim God has spoken is one which He indeed has spoken, then we should believe with our whole heart that we will receive the blessings. Anything less than this would be a resolve to live beneath one's privilege. Yet while enjoying the blessings, let us not neglect to be quick to use them to bless God in turn, by using them to advance the cause of Christ. Now there will be doubters looking on along the way; but they come with the territory. So go ahead and be "ridiculous." You will be perceived that way anyway. Again, be "ridiculous." Only in being "ridiculous" in our faith will we obtain the promises of God. Since faith requires doing the "ridiculous," let us do precisely that!

Principle Four

Faith begins where human ability ends

"By faith Sarah herself also received strength to conceive seed, and she bore a child when she was past the age, because she judged Him faithful who had promised. Therefore from one man, and him as good as dead, were born as many as the stars of the sky in multitude—innumerable as the sand which is by the seashore."

Heb 11:11–12

As we leave the previous principle and begin to discuss the next, the transition between the two stories should, I believe, help give the reader an even greater appreciation for the inspiration of the word of God than may have been had prior to considering the principles. In the last principle we understood that faith requires doing the "ridiculous." We put the word ridiculous in quotations to underscore the fact that the idea behind describing faith as being ridiculous is to provide a way of explaining the perception of doubters who question the faith of others. In turning to this next principle, we now see one of the main reasons for such perception: failure to accept the fact that faith is the substance that continues the journey just at the point where human strength has failed!

In truth, not only does faith continue the journey at this point, but faith can only begin here—the place where all human efforts prove futile to accomplish what God has decreed. We can say our father and mother in the faith, Abraham and Sarah, learned this well. From the time we are introduced to Abram and Sarai, whose names would later be changed to Abraham and Sarah respectively, in Genesis 11, we are told they were without children and Sarai was also barren. But as part of the incentive to believe God to get up and leave his country, Abram was told the good news that he would be blessed with children, so much so that they would be innumerable. At this point, we are also told that Abram was a staggering seventy-five years old with his wife being just ten years younger and beyond the age of child bearing. Then, as if it would not have been a great enough miracle for them to have had seed at that stage in their lives, God prolonged the promise for another twenty-five years, which signified not only the death of their reproductive systems, but the virtual ineligibility of the patriarch and the matriarch for receiving a miracle with respect to giving birth to a child, from a human point of view, that is. But this was the point which was absolutely necessary that they got to—the place where human ability was powerless to achieve the promise—in order for the miracle to truly have been by faith. Talk about "ridiculous"!

Furthermore, since sexual relations were required for conception to take place, it was necessary that the story unfolded the way it did in order to rule out the possibility of anyone, including Abraham and Sarah, being able to rationalize the miracle scientifically as being a human accomplishment. This observation thus highlights yet another dimension of human abilities that must also be exhausted before faith truly begins to take effect, namely, human reasoning. Faith marks not only the end of human strength to accomplish results, but also the end of humans' ability to conceptualize possibilities of doing so. Whenever anyone claims to be able to explain the manner in which God will bring about a miracle simply by reasoning, we can be certain that such explanation is not of God. This truth was exemplified in Abraham and Sarah's attempt to produce the seed. God's promised seed was Isaac, but after taking into account the deadness of Sarah's reproductive system, though they initially believed, over time, they ruled out the possibility of the seed coming through her. Then, as an alternative, in agreement with Sarah's suggestion, Abraham took Sarah's maid, Hagar, to be his wife, and she conceived a son (Gen 16:1-4). But instead of the promised child, Ishmael was born, and it was not long after that Sarah realized that he was not the promised seed. Consequently, it is evident that what was planned by human reasoning was not according to faith. Now the same is true today and will always be the case!

What should one suppose will be the thought if a matter is resolved with the help of any measure of human intellect, no matter how small that might be? No doubt, especially given the arrogance and haughtiness that is often displayed by many of us, we may predict that there would be a strong possibility, if not a guarantee, that someone would be inclined to assume the credit. In light of this likelihood, I believe God ordained it that virtually by definition, faith can only truly be faith when that which it brings about takes place only after all human methods of attempting to do the same are exhausted. To add further emphasis to this notion, let us take another look at the fundamental truth about faith given in the opening verse of Hebrews 11. There we learn that *"faith is the substance of things hoped for."* Since faith is what gives us confidence for the things we hope for in God, it should be evident that the one who hopes for the thing actually has no control, power, or influence whatsoever, to bring the thing into existence. Rather, hope is dependent on another—the other being God. God, in turn, has gifted us with a tool to enable us to realize our hopes—faith. If, by chance, however, hope should be dependent in any way on the one doing the hoping, then that "hope" is no longer truly hope at all but human achievement. In such scenario it would be justifiable to attribute praise to the individual who does the accomplishing; but since God will have no part in anything of the like, all possibility of human enabling—both physical and mental—must come to an end before faith steps in and becomes the means by which hope comes to fruition.

Invariably, when faith causes hope to materialize, the fact of faith being the cause of such effect need not be argued to proponents or opponents of the concept of faith alike. An example of this truth is the story of the healing of the man with the withered hand (Mark 3:1-6). The deformity was visible and undeniable to all. It was also clear that there was nothing anyone could do to restore that arm like the other. Correction, there was actually someone who could do it, Jesus the Christ, the Son of God. When Christ eventually healed the man of the condition, not even His enemies were able to deny that a bona fide miracle had taken place through faith. And since they could not conceive of any possible explanation to discredit the working of faith, the only thing His adversaries could do in response was to complain about the timing of the miracle since it was done on the Sabbath. What was convincing to all was that Jesus, who possessed the faith of God to perfection (Mark 11:12-24), performed the deed through faith when all human possibilities were ineffective. And what can we say about the admission of the Sanhedrin, which opposed Peter and John following the healing of the man who was born lame (Acts 3:1-10)? Though the elders opposed them, in response to the event, they exclaimed, *"What shall we do to these men? For, indeed, that a notable miracle has been done through them is evident to all who dwell in Jerusalem, and we cannot deny it"* (Acts 4:16). Because it was clear that no mortal strength could have brought about such effect, it was undeniable that faith was the only means whereby it was accomplished.

Not only in the examples of Scripture, however, should we be able to note examples where it was undeniable that faith was at work instead of human intervention. We should also be able to recall various moments in our lives when we knew that all hope was lost as we were faced with an assortment of trials. Perhaps it was a bill that was due and there were going to be dire consequences if it was not paid by a certain date; yet we found ourselves at the due date having no means of acquiring the finances. Then suddenly, seemingly out of nowhere, we miraculously came into possession of the necessary amount. Or, it may have been a situation where we or our loved ones were deserving of punishment for some wrong-doing; but instead of judgment, mercy was obtained. Likewise, there are surely countless other similar examples that can be brought to mind where in every case, due to both the timing and the manner in which deliverance and victory was experienced, it was clear that we experienced them by faith, and by faith alone. This is the state of affairs whenever faith is truly at work.

Because we are rational beings, the truth of the timing of faith in relation to the end of our strength has perhaps been extremely difficult for many to embrace, ever since this truth was first revealed millennia ago. Most of us today, especially the intellectual and the scientific, find it difficult to impossible to embrace any other options than those which can be explained in logical or scientific terms. An outline of the steps leading to the final outcome, which can be proven upon experimentation at every point, must be provided if there is to be any belief in either a prediction by faith or an already performed miracle through faith. When this is not furnished, it leads to doubt and the pursuit of comprehensible solutions and explanations; and since, according to the truth revealed in the present principle, such comprehensible solutions and explanations are not of God, but are human in origin, they prove to be futile to either bring about the promise of God, or to explain what God has already done.

FAITH AND WORKS

The point where faith takes over from all human efforts and abilities also emphasizes a most important distinction between faith and works. Works speak of human doings whereas faith denotes that which is wrought by God. To rely upon works signifies either the ignoring of faith or worse, the denial of the power of faith. We will soon discuss the type of works which James spoke of in James 2 that must be demonstrated in conjunction with faith; but for now it will be asserted that whenever works are rendered in substitution for faith, it is a sign of either an ignoring of faith or a denial of its power. Such works, whenever they accomplish anything, cause praise to be directed to the one by whose hands they were performed. But God is absolutely unwilling to share praise and glory with anyone, so He waits until all such human efforts are exhausted, then steps in so that it should be known beyond the shadow of a doubt that His hands were at work in the situation to bring about the miraculous outcome.

To illustrate the infinite chasm between faith and works, not only does God wait until all human efforts have been exhausted and proven futile to accomplish His will, but God also exposes the "fruit" of works for all involved and those looking on to see, prior to allowing faith to bring about His purpose. As an example of this, let us take another look at the story of Abraham and Sarah in Genesis 16. By the works of the flesh, Ishmael was conceived because Abraham and Sarah initially failed to look past what was evident to the natural eyes in terms of the deadness of their reproductive systems and trust God absolutely to bring about the promise He made to them. Then notice how God allowed them to see the error of their way to demonstrate the futility of the works of the flesh. First, immediately after Hagar conceived, she despised Sarai; and upon realizing this, Sarai confronted Abram about their wrong-doing, which was essentially the utilization of fleshly methods to obtain the promise that God had previously sworn by Himself to fulfill. Next, to compound the issue, after Isaac—the son of promise— was born and was weaned and received a great feast from his father, Sarah observed Ishmael laughing at Isaac. At this point, Sarah had seen enough and this time insisted that Abraham send Hagar and Ishmael away. When Abraham was displeased with Sarah's demand, God Himself stepped in and commanded Abraham to heed his wife's advice (Gen 21:8–21).

What both Abraham and Sarah experienced was the byproduct of works done in substitution for faith in God. The consequence was utter frustration, and such is still the case whenever works are utilized as the means of achieving promised blessing. This byproduct is characterized by several undesirable effects, reminiscent of those that resulted when the seed according to the flesh was produced. First, even well before birth, and as early as the time of conception, reality set in—the impatience in not waiting for God to produce the seed was not worth it. Hagar despised her mistress. The provision that was thought would bring peace actually brought strife. Instead of bringing happiness, sadness and anguish accompanied the seed. The apostle Paul later shed light on exactly what is at work in such instances. In commenting on the contention between the promised seed and the seed according to the flesh, Paul noted the core of the problem, *"But, as he who was born according to the flesh then persecuted him who was born according to the Spirit, even so it is now"* (Gal 4:29). The heart of the matter is that the flesh and the Spirit are constantly at war with each other and the two can never agree (Gal 5:17). Whenever we engage the works of the flesh, then, we will always become frustrated, because when faith, which is according to the Spirit, takes effect, the byproducts of both will collide, just as it happened for Abraham and Sarah.

The only recourse at this point, just as Sarah realized, is to remove the source of persecution far from us. The thing that was once so longed for now became a thorn in the side. Abraham was left with the difficult but necessary task of having to send Hagar and Ishmael away. Note however, that was not the end of the story for Ishmael, because God promised to make a nation of him since he was also Abraham's child, although not the one in whom the Seed, namely, Christ, would be called (Gen 21:13; Gal 3:16). A big concern though was the prediction concerning the nature of the man Ishmael—he was to be a wild man who would oppose every man (Gen 16:12); and yes, Isaac was not to be excluded from those whom Ishmael would oppose. This was soon realized when Ishmael scoffed at Isaac as soon as he was weaned; and even to this day, the descendants of Isaac and those of Ishmael are at enmity with each other. This demonstrates the horrible consequence of employing the methods of the flesh instead of those of the Spirit, which are through faith.

So, as we look back over many of our experiences in life when we not only seemed to run into brick walls but the walls seemingly fought back against us creating much frustration and grief, whereas in times past it may have been a mystery why such was the case, now that we have this renewed perspective, the cloud of confusion should no longer hang over us. All along we suffered the consequence of reaping the fruits of our efforts exerted according to fleshly methods to accomplish those things which only faith could make possible. We often reasoned, researched, brainstormed, and even consulted with others who were supposed to be wise and knowledgeable in the areas of dilemmas which we faced. If the truth be told, those moments may also be characterized as times during which our prayer lives were at their strongest. Just think back for a moment on some of the difficult decisions you wrestled with even in recent times: moments such as when you worried and became stressed over how certain bills would be paid; how to handle a rebellious child or an unloving spouse; or some other difficult decision in which there was a timeline and the deadline was fast approaching. For example, your job was perhaps about to relocate to another state and the decision had to be made whether to uproot your family along with everything else that goes with that action, and what about the ensuing struggle you faced over the uncertainty of how the final decision would benefit or hurt your family? No doubt we can all recall numerous other examples, some of which may have been quite unique; but in every case we note, the dilemma was the same: what should I do?

As people of faith, it is highly likely that the testimony of having prayed and believed God for the answer during each of those moments is one we may all claim to have. But while our testimonies may not be disputable, what is certain is the record of our poor display of patience during those moments in not allowing faith to have opportunity to be the channel through which the answer should come. This is evident from the trail of frustration which none of us is without in our history of making difficult decisions. We prayed and believed, but as the time and intensity increased, the temptation to resort to works—the solutions of the flesh—became too overwhelming, so we often yielded, and then the fruits of those measures soon followed in the form of frustration and distress. Hopefully, the lesson now learned is that no matter how desperate the situation, faith must be acknowledged and employed in the circumstance. Often when we work out the solution to our problems, it appears to be the right way to proceed; but later when such methods are exposed as being inadequate to accomplish what is necessary, we realize what they truly were all along—works of the flesh. This is the risk we face even following the most diligent journey toward discovering the solution, whether it is consulting the wisest minds on the matter or exerting all of our mental and physical energy to determine it. In the end, instead of discovering the answer, we find confusion and frustration as we sink deeper into despair.

Considering this reality, one should not need further convincing of the benefit of waiting for faith, in its proper time, to have opportunity to bring to fruition the will of God. This should be apparent when we note the joy brought to Abraham and Sarah upon receiving the seed according to promise—in contrast to what resulted when the seed according to the flesh was conceived. When the promised child was born, Abraham named him Isaac, meaning "laughter"; and in response, Sarah exclaimed, "'*God has made me laugh, and all who hear will laugh with me.*' *She also said, 'Who would have said to Abraham that Sarah would nurse children? For I have borne him a son in his old age'*" (Gen 21:6-7). This gesture on their part in naming the seed according to faith as they did epitomizes what we can expect when we wait on God: peace, overflowing joy, and laughter! Who said God does not have a sense of humor? Also notice, the writer made it clear that Sarah bore Abraham the child "*at the set time of which God had spoken to him*" that it would happen (Gen 21:2). This proves both the sureness of the promises of God and how impossible it is for fleshly methods to bring them to pass. If God makes a promise, He is more than able to fulfill it in His own time!

OUR ROLE AND FAITH

While the point may be sufficiently argued by now, there still remain important questions that are left unanswered. First, does all that has been said mean we are to neglect all human senses, reasoning, and intuition when faced with challenges and decision making in our lives? Secondly, how do we reconcile the notion that works are inadequate to accomplish what only faith can—with James' assertion that *"faith without works is dead"* (Jas 2:26), which clearly signifies the importance of works for faith? To answer the first question, certainly not! In contrast to the animals that behave based on instinct, God created humans with the ability to reason. We were created as intelligent, rational beings and we are expected by God to behave that way. As such, we should make responsible decisions—some of which will be difficult at times and others not as difficult—on a moment by moment basis. Because we are intelligent beings, unless the occasion for making a decision is one requiring quick reflex action, our decisions should be made only following careful thinking and taking into consideration the experiences of others as well as our own, observing trends, considering the suggestions of others, and factoring a whole host of other variables into the process. God created us with the ability to reason, and not only does God expect us to use our rationality, but He also holds us accountable for the decisions we make.

Yet there are times when God decrees promises, as He did to Abraham and Sarah, and faith is the *only* key able to unlock the door to those promises, from both a conceptual and a physical standpoint. Remember the assertion of the writer of Hebrews in the first verse of chapter 11: *"faith is the substance of things hoped for, the evidence of things not seen."* An obvious implication of the statement is that the things hoped for are those hoped for in God. In other words, those promised by God, whether salvation, healing, deliverance, or the like. Also note the use of the verb "to be" as well as the definite article "the": *"faith is the . . ."* This means there is simply no other substance of things hoped for or other evidence of things not seen—besides faith—which can procure the promises of God. Problems therefore surface, like what Abraham and Sarah experienced when Ishmael was conceived, when we substitute other ways and means for faith in an attempt to bring those promises to pass. This is where our best efforts, both physical and mental, fall short. Once again, just remember Abraham and Sarah, and the point should be obvious.

This now leaves us with the other question: how do we reconcile the truth about the futility of works to accomplish the promises of God with the assertion of James that *"faith without works is dead"* (Jas 2:26)? Since faith is so powerful to accomplish so much, how can it be said to be useless apart from works or, even worse, dead? To understand the point made by James, special attention should be given to v. 22 of James 2, where the argument is found. By using the example of Abraham, when he heeded God's command to sacrifice Isaac, the son of promise, James pointed out that it was Abraham's works in conjunction with his faith that made his faith complete. Abraham could have said he believed God all he wanted and called that belief faith; yet the only way of knowing if such belief was authentic was to see it acting out what it professed, which meant following through with the action of performing the sacrifice. Such action in obedience to the word of God is the type of work James spoke of as being necessary to accompany faith to make it complete. Accordingly, it was upon his demonstration of this type of work to the point where God had to call out to him from heaven to terminate the motion begun to slay his son, that Abraham was justified and assured the promise of posterity. Thus he was justified not only because he had faith, but because he acted upon that faith.

The kind of works that are said to be inadequate to obtain the promises of God therefore are entirely different to those spoken of by James as being necessary to accompany faith. The former are engaged as substitutes for faith. Those are the type which the apostle Paul spoke out against because by them many thought they could obtain justification—the most important promise of God—when only faith can do this (see Romans 4 and Galatians 3). On the other hand, the works of which James spoke ought to be a natural outflow of what one is convinced of in the heart by faith. The misunderstanding of the difference between the arguments by Paul and James can lead to confusion, so it is important to understand the context of both. This misunderstanding caused the reformer, Martin Luther, to promote the marginalization of James because he thought James contradicted Paul in attempting to advance the observance of the Law instead of faith.[1] It is clear however that the two did not contradict each other at all—but were addressing two different issues. Paul addressed the folly of those who thought works could be used as a substitute for faith unto justification while James addressed the hypocrisy of those who said they had faith but failed to demonstrate their faith by performing the deeds that should flow naturally from faith to make it complete. James' argument now sheds even greater light on the first principle where we learned that faith must be based on the word of God. If faith is indeed based on the word of God and we believe the word, then we act upon it. Otherwise, how can we say we truly believe? Separated from these works, one's "faith" is dead! Such "faith" simply will not accomplish anything.

Just as we see in the example of Abraham, when we believe God for His promises, there will be actions expected of us to complete the work already begun by faith in us, of providing hope in the face of mounting obstacles and seeming impossibilities. The reality of this truth should be quite evident if we look back over many of our experiences. For example, while we were unemployed, God may have assured us of an employment opportunity. This assurance provided hope in the midst of despair. Still,

---

1. Johnson, "James," 197.

there were some obvious actions that were required for us to perform in order to make the promise a reality. These included updating our resumes, filling out applications, and appearing for job interviews. Such actions represent performing the works that should flow naturally out of the faith one professes to have. Without these works, it can be easily argued that there was an absence of faith in the first place to believe that the promise was guaranteed.

NATURE OF THE WORKS THAT ACCOMPANY FAITH

Having now explored the relationship between works and real faith, I think it is important to discuss also, in detail, the nature of the works which must accompany faith in order for us to strive to do them, thereby ensuring our reception of the things for which we hope. In attempting to do this, I believe there is perhaps no better way to search for this understanding than to "consult" the one who argued the point in the first place, namely, James. Among all of the available examples in Scripture where it could be demonstrated that it is ultimately one's works in conjunction with his or her faith that leads to justification, James chose the examples of Abraham and Rahab to convey this. His choices appear to have been motivated precisely by his observation of some characteristics of their works, which he thought should be highlighted as lessons for his readers. Doing likewise will be necessary if we expect to receive the kind of results those two enjoyed. As we shall see, although it was revealed to them in different ways, in both cases, each acted in obedience to the word of God as they heard it, because they believed.

In acting upon the word, which they heard and believed, both demonstrated different aspects of real faith in action that always "move" God. First, in looking at the example of Abraham, from what we learn about him from the story in Genesis 22 and from other passages, he had an intimate relationship with God. He received a special calling from God to be the father of God's chosen people, a people chosen to represent God on earth. Those people, as we know, were to come through Abraham's descendant, Isaac. But in a strange twist in the story, God spoke to Abraham, instructing Him to offer up Isaac as a burnt offering. And he was commanded to do this long before Isaac had opportunity to extend the lineage; thus making it a call to cut off the promise. This was a specific word to Abraham, and a difficult one, to say the least! Still, Abraham set out to obey the word of the Lord. The narrator tells us it was meant to be a test from God, but evidently Abraham was not privy to this information. As we read the story in Genesis, upon receiving the instruction, without hesitation, Abraham rose early the next morning, setting out on the journey to the mountain appointed by God for the sacrifice, taking along two servants, a donkey carrying the wood he had prepared for the sacrifice, as well as the sacrifice himself, that is, Isaac. Then we are told it was after three days of journeying that Abraham finally saw the place from afar off, where the sacrifice was to be made. This last detail in the story highlights a very important characteristic of Abraham's action: it was enduring and persistent; indeed one that demonstrated what it meant to stay the course.

While it was commendable that his action was without hesitation in that he delayed for only the time necessary to gather what was needed for the journey; what was even more commendable was his continuance of the journey for three days before arriving at his destination. During the course of those three days, though the story does not mention it, Abraham no doubt wrestled within himself, as any of us would be expected to, over the thought of what God told him to do. In analyzing this strong possibility, we first take note of the love he had for his son, which was a fact that God even reminded him of (Gen 22:2). Secondly, though Ishmael was also his son, the promise was through Isaac, which is evidently why he was called his only son; and if slaughtered, the promise would not materialize. Thirdly, what father would want to tie his son to an altar, slay him, and then set him on fire, even if as a burnt offering to the Lord? Despite these and numerous other possible thoughts that must have flowed through Abraham's mind over the course of what must have been the three most difficult days of his life, Abraham stayed the course with one purpose in mind—to obey the word of God! What faith; and even more remarkably, what works that accompanied such faith! He did not allow emotion or even intellect to get in the way of his obedience of the word of God.

If Abraham expected to receive the end of his faith, and he did, it was not going to be the initial "jump" of obedience, although it was without hesitation, which would complete his faith. If he had aborted the journey on the second day or turned back on the third, the story would have been told quite differently, and James would perhaps use his example only for the purpose of teaching his readers what not to do. Conversely, it was his persistence in staying the course for as long as the journey required, up to and including the final action, that made his faith complete. Accordingly, an important characteristic of works performed in faith is: it must be enduring for as long as necessary. To abandon the journey, no matter how close we come to the end, apart from the grace of God intervening to allow for some other way, would mean failure to see the promise.

Upon arrival at the place for sacrifice and seeing all the necessary components for the offering except the sacrifice, Isaac asked his father where the lamb was. To this question, Abraham cleverly redirected the responsibility of providing it to God saying, *"My son, God will provide for Himself the lamb for a burnt offering"* (Gen 22:8). This next aspect of the story brings us to yet another essential attribute of the works that must accompany faith. Without having to do any works whatsoever, faith can be rather "shallow," in that it can be kept in the heart and concealed from others. On the other hand, when actions are required, faith is exposed for all to see. This reality points us to the next feature that must characterize our actions that support our faith, which Abraham also demonstrated: our actions must withstand scrutiny. If they fail to do so, we will most certainly abandon the journey. We have already considered the scrutiny Abraham overcame from within, but now this next level of scrutiny came from someone else. Although we read only of his being questioned by his son, this is certainly not to say it is not reasonable to assume that his wife, who was left at home, did not also have questions, as well as the two servants who traveled with them for three days. Still, Abraham obviously overcame it all since he came to the point of being in the act of attempting to slay his son, until God intervened.

To withstand scrutiny does not mean we will always have answers to give to those who ask us the "hows" and "whys" about God's word, which He speaks to us. What it does mean is that despite the scrutiny, there should remain such an assurance in our hearts of the word of God that we will persevere, no matter how skeptical others may be. Furthermore, not only will one's actions be questioned, but invariably the questions will move far beyond the point of just being questions and to the extent of our being ridiculed. But even so, we must remain firm. We must remember that these reactions are to be expected because, as we may recall from the previous principle of faith, what we do will always appear to be ridiculous to most. Understandably, despite this awareness, it is quite trying to keep one's focus when others oppose us, especially for prolonged periods. Nevertheless, this is what is required of us. Imagine what Noah endured while building the ark in the middle of nowhere and gathering animals in obedience to the word of God, while he and his family had to endure mocking by everyone else. Scrutiny and derision comes with having faith in God, but acting upon that belief, withstanding the scorn, and remaining assured in our hearts while doing what God has commanded us to do, demonstrates our faith.

So Abraham persisted in the face of questioning from his son and proceeded to do what God instructed him to do. Then coming to the moment of the final act of faith, he passed the last and ultimate test of determination to carry out the command by motioning to slay his son, which was just as good as if he committed the act. Upon seeing this gesture, God, who was obviously satisfied with Abraham's actions to that point, intervened by calling out to him from heaven to halt the action. Then after this intervention came the declaration from God to the point that He swore by Himself to bless Abraham saying, *"By Myself I have sworn, says the Lord, because you have done this thing, and have not withheld your son, your only son—blessing I will bless you, and multiplying I will multiply your descendants..."* (Gen 22:16–17). Finally, as credence to what James taught about works and faith, it is interesting to note that the Lord did not focus here on what Abraham believed as being the occasion for the blessing, but on what he had done, thus indicating it was his works, which emanated from his faith, that ultimately led to his blessing.

As a final note about Abraham's actions, I think an important point needs to be made about God's command to him to avoid the possible misunderstanding that God might today call us to offer up another human being as a sacrifice. While it is clear from the story that Abraham was unaware that the command was really a test of his faith, such unawareness should not be said of us, because the narrator explicitly stated that it was a test. Noted Biblical scholar, Thomas W. Mann, provides an insightful discussion about the likely reasons why God saw the need to test Abraham in this most difficult manner.[2] All along, God did not intend for Abraham to complete the sacrifice, but wanted to determine his faithfulness to Him. As such, one should not walk away from reading this story intending to cite it as justification for offering up another human being as a sacrifice to God, for any reason. In fact, because Christ's sacrifice was sufficient to satisfy God's righteous requirement of atonement for sin, although Abraham did offer up a ram as a burnt offering in the end, not even offering animal

---

2. Mann, *Torah*, 44–48.

sacrifice in our present day can be justified from the story. So while this story of Abraham's obedience should inspire us to faithful obedience to God, it should be clear that just as God did not expect Abraham to offer up his son as a sacrifice, God will not ask any of us to offer up another human being as a sacrifice.

Now as opposed to Abraham who acted in response to a specific address from God, Rahab the harlot—the other person referred to by James as an example of demonstrating faith being completed by works—did not receive a specific address from God. Instead, she took faith to another level by taking the initiative to embrace a general understanding about God by faith, and then acted on it. We will deal more specifically with Rahab later, in principle number nine, but for now her actions draw attention to several key qualities that should depict works done in faith. As we see in the story in Joshua 2, two spies went down to survey Jericho, and while there, lodged in Rahab's house. Upon learning of their stay at her house, the king of Jericho sent to her, asking her to turn them over to the authorities. But remarkably, although the spies had made her no promises, because she feared God more than she did the king, Rahab disobeyed the king's order and hid the men, excusing that they had escaped. She then deceived the authorities, misleading them to take her advice to pursue the men outside the gates of the city; and after some time when the pursuers had gone, she let them go. Her actions were most commendable in that she was not an Israelite and yet she believed and acted upon what she had heard about God, trusting that ultimately God, not the spies, would spare her life and her family's. Notice also that her actions came before she received the assurance from the spies that she would be spared. No doubt she must have heard that the God of the Hebrews was a gracious and merciful God who would hear a humble cry; and though He did not speak this to her specifically, she embraced that truth, put her whole trust in it, and acted upon it because she feared God more than the king.

This quality of Rahab's actions therefore was one in which initiative was displayed. So, like Rahab, we must be willing to act upon the revealed truth in God's word without waiting for a "specific" word, such as a prophecy or word of knowledge, to be spoken directly to us. Once we know the revealed truth in God's word, God honors every effort we put forth to obey it. This is why James, in laying the foundation for his argument of why faith was dead without works, asked the question of how we can see a brother or a sister who is destitute of food and not act to relieve the person's suffering, merely telling him or her to depart in peace and be filled and warmed (Jas 2:14–17). According to Matt 25:31–46, whenever we show benevolence to anyone who is in need, Christ considers it to be an act of kindness done to Him. If so, we should take the initiative and go beyond saying depart and be filled and warmed—and provide the need if it is in our power to do so, or at least help direct the individual to such help if we ourselves are unable to provide it. In such cases we should not wait for a "word" to instruct us to feed the hungry and to clothe the naked; but just like Rahab, we must spontaneously perform the necessary works to cause what we believe to become a reality, even if it is on the behalf of another.

Another noteworthy feature of Rahab's actions was that she did not act out of selfish ambition. She proved this by not pleading for her own her life only, but also for the lives of her loved ones. Potentially, we can be diligent in our efforts, which we perform in faith, but in the process also fall short of considering how others can benefit from the blessings we will ultimately receive. For example, yes we are the ones in need of a job, but is there any intention of being a blessing to someone else once we receive it? Without question, God is pleased when we endeavor to share with others the blessings which He bestows on us, for the Scripture says, *"It is more blessed to give than to receive"* (Acts 20:35). Many of us wallow in our blessings and we justify our selfishness in the process by saying, "I worked hard for this." But while this is true and we should not have to defend our right to enjoying the fruit of our labor, do we ever stop to consider that we were also blessed in order to be a blessing to others? We are channels of blessings. As such, the blessings of God should not find their final resting place with us but should also, at least in part, be transferred to others. Rahab demonstrated works that were not performed out of selfish ambition, and her example should serve as a model for us in all we do by faith.

One last very important attribute of Rahab's works was the care she displayed in following every detail for securing deliverance, which the spies instructed her to observe. To hide them and later set them free was exemplary, yet it was only the first step. In order to secure deliverance for herself and for her loved ones when the city would be overtaken, she needed to follow some important instructions completely. The matter was to be kept secret; she was to bind a provided scarlet cord in her window; she was to bring all her loved ones to her house; and they were to remain there until rescued. Rahab followed every detail, and when the city was overrun by Joshua and his troops, her whole household was spared because of her complete obedience. This quality, in addition to the attribute of endurance displayed by Abraham in continuing his journey after many days, emphasizes that it is not enough to begin the journey, or even to continue it, but there must also be careful observance to do everything we are commanded to do, every step of the way.

When we perform the works necessary for faith, we must be careful to observe every aspect of those works or we jeopardize the fulfillment of the promises of God. There is a frightening example in the word of God that speaks to this issue involving someone, who, as opposed to Rahab, chose to ignore some very important details of a mission that was committed to his trust to carry out in favor of doing only those aspects he considered to be necessary to perform. That individual was King Saul. His example of a lack of complete obedience is one from which we should learn; we may well suffer similar severe consequences if we act as he did. The story is told in 1 Samuel 15, where Saul received instruction from God through the prophet Samuel to destroy utterly the Amalekites in retaliation for their ambush against the Israelites when they came out of Egypt (see, also, Deut 25:17–19). Saul was explicitly told not to spare anyone or anything, including livestock. Still, unwilling to destroy everything, he spared the king, the best of the livestock, and everything that was good. Even worse, when asked by Samuel whether he had carried out the command, he lied, not knowing that God had already informed the prophet of his disobedience. Moreover, when Samuel heard the noise of the sheep that were spared and questioned him about it, he blamed the people for sparing them, saying they had done so in order to sacrifice them unto the Lord. After giving this final poor response to the prophet's inquiry, then came the terrible reality for Saul: because of his disobedience, the Lord rejected him from being king over Israel any longer and chose another, namely, David, to reign in his place.

The story of Saul's failure possibly raises an important concern: is there cruelty and lack of compassion in God? Rather than interpreting the events of this story to mean this is how God judges communities in general, however, it might be helpful to take the background of the story into consideration, so that God's commands to King Saul may be understood as being more confined to this occasion than being the norm. Biblical scholar, Bruce C. Birch, notes that, at stake in the story, "is not Saul's violation of a norm for holy war. It is, instead, his failure to carry out the explicit command of the Lord . . . on this occasion."[3] God had sworn to Moses and the children of Israel that He would punish the Amalekites for their cowardly act against the Israelites when they left Egypt, and now it was King Saul's responsibility to carry it out. Not only was this command retribution for that prior offense, but also a remedy for a persistent problem (see 1 Sam 14:48). As severe as it was, it was one that God, in His justice, determined was necessary. Nevertheless, it was not the norm then, and even more importantly, Scripture gives clear indication that it is not in effect today—see, for example, Christ's command to love everyone, even our enemies (Matt 5:43–48).

At any rate, failing to perform every detail as the Lord commands us to as Saul did is ultimately an indication of a lack of faith in the word of God, no matter the form it comes to us. It is a statement to God that we really do not believe Him when He makes a promise. This explains our failure to obey, and in failing to obey, we disqualify ourselves from receiving the blessing. This fact is obvious since our works are necessary to make our faith complete and faith in turn is the key that unlocks the promise; but if our works are ineffective, our faith is incomplete, and the promise is not able to come to pass. Imagine what would have happened if Rahab kept secret the matter of the spies, brought her entire family to her house, and kept them inside until the conquest, but failed to hang the scarlet cord from her window. Should she have expected to be spared if such were the case? Certainly she should not! In the same way, if, like King Saul, we perform only some of the works that are required to make faith complete, we should not expect to receive the promises of God also. Being careful to follow every detail accordingly, in addition to the other characteristics demonstrated by Abraham and Rahab, should bespeak our works that naturally flow out of our faith, if we expect our faith to be complete.

The assertion that *"Faith without works is dead"* is an irrefutable truth. But not any kind of works will fit into this equation. Yes we might say we believe God's word and are working by faith to bring it to pass; but our works will be ineffective if they are not of the caliber of those performed by Abraham and Rahab. If we truly believe, we will produce works that not only conform to the moral and ethical standards of the word of God, but ones that also display a deep level of endurance, thereby ensuring triumph in our faith. Such was the testimony of our ancestors,

---

3. Birch, "Samuel," 1087.

Abraham and Rahab, and we can be certain of it being ours as well, if we learn from their examples.

A FINAL WORD

At the outset, the assertion that faith can only begin where human ability ends may have been unsettling to some. Many of us perhaps like to call attention to our strengths and accomplishments. Although we might be mindful to tack on phrases such as "by the grace of God" or "to God be the glory," when we make mention of them, we must be careful to examine our hearts, because God will not share His glory with anyone. Our capabilities may be undeniable, but the fact remains, without allowing God to work through us to accomplish His will by faith, none of our abilities will ever be sufficient to accomplish God's will on earth. At the very least, then, we should thank God for blessing us with all of our abilities that we are able to use to perform the necessary works to make our faith complete. For even in the possession of those abilities we should acknowledge the providence of God in choosing to bestow them on us. Consequently, we should be careful never to be so haughty as to fail to give God the glory for every step of the journey, which we take toward the promise, because providence grace is at work in every one of those steps.

I am aware of the likelihood that what I have suggested might be a humbling thing for some to consider; nonetheless, I assert, it is one which every believer should come to embrace. Everything we do in our own strength, as opposed to relying on faith to bring about the promises of God, will ultimately end in frustration, exhaustion, and futility. But when we labor, doing what our faith requires to make it complete, we can do so with the assurance of victory because we put our whole trust in God. This trust is precisely what enables us to feel at rest in Him and not stressed. So no longer will the idea that faith signifies the endpoint of our abilities be disconcerting to those of us who like to feel like we are always in control. On the contrary, it will be a comforting joy to know that we no longer have to wrestle in our minds, trying to figure out how we can obtain the promises of God. Let us therefore strive to walk in faith, wholeheartedly trusting God knowing that, if He promised, He will perform. Only what He commissions us to do by faith will we do. And when we do this, we have the assurance, not only that we will receive the promise, but also that it will come to us while we rest in God.

Principle Five

Faith ultimately works toward preparing us for our heavenly home

> *"By faith Abraham obeyed when he was called to go out to the place which he would receive as an inheritance. And he went out, not knowing where he was going. By faith he dwelt in the land of promise as in a foreign country, dwelling in tents with Isaac and Jacob, the heirs with him of the same promise; for he waited for the city which has foundations, whose builder and maker is God. . . .*
>
> *These all died in faith, not having received the promises, but having seen them afar off were assured of them, embraced them and confessed that they were strangers and pilgrims on the earth. For those who say such things declare plainly that they seek a homeland. And truly if they had called to mind that country from which they had come out, they would have had opportunity to return. But now they desire a better, that is, a heavenly country. Therefore God is not ashamed to be called their God, for He has prepared a city for them."*
>
> Heb 11:8–10, 13–16

This section of Scripture recounts the story in Genesis 12, involving the call of Abraham from his homeland to an unfamiliar country, which he would receive as an inheritance. Abraham, we are told, immediately trusted God for the promise and set out on the journey to receive his promise. Now if we are honest, we should admit that these few details in the retelling of the story thus far line up quite nicely with much of the overtones that characterize some of today's teachings on faith. That is to say, just as land was promised to Abraham, in those teachings something is also emphasized as being promised to us as our inheritance. The promise might be prosperity, healing, favor, or the like; and as a result, we can now have joy in knowing that it is ours if we have faith enough to believe it. But interestingly, it is also from this same point where one might be quick to get excited in the Hebrews account, where an obvious and sudden shift in direction takes place from where the reader might expect the writer to take him to somewhere else totally unexpected. Instead of continuing to retell the story, the writer's focus shifted to interpreting the motive of the patriarch for following through with such a revolutionary act as to relocate from a place of familiarity and seeming comfort, to sojourn as a stranger in a foreign land of which he was absolutely unfamiliar and unaware of what the conditions there would be. Clearly his motive was something more important than simply to inherit land, and the writer wanted to convey this to his readers

To explain the ultimate motive of the patriarch, both in verses ten and sixteen the writer made it clear that Abraham ultimately looked for a city that was not of this world! It was a city that no mortal could build. A very important description of the city, we are told, is that it has foundations, with the implication being that they are immovable, because God Himself is the architect and constructor of the city. It is a city like none other Abraham had seen or could have imagined. Now as we consider this, we should be careful not to think that the writer intended to allegorize the story as if Abraham did not truly go out looking for an earthly city to dwell in, as God told him to. For indeed, God took him to the place and told him to look all around him for all he would see would be his and his descendants' forever. Moreover, he was told to walk its length and width, thus indicating the land had a real geographical location on earth (Gen 13:14–18). So the intent of the writer of Hebrews was clearly in no way to deny this reality; rather, it was to suggest that the piece of real estate was not the ultimate home Abraham searched for, but a heavenly one. His motive for sojourning was not only his hope of receiving the earthly inheritance; but beyond that, based on his relationship with God, he hoped for a greater inheritance, that is, one out of this world, in the heavenly domain. Though he had faith to believe in the earthly promise, then, his faith aimed much higher onto the heavenly promise.

Hebrews 12 begins by encouraging the reader to follow the example of the witnesses like Abraham who have gone on before us running the race to the finish line, following Jesus who prepared the way for everyone and is also now seated at the right hand of God. Thus Abraham, like the other witnesses, ran the race toward the finish line that was nowhere to be found on earth, but in glory. That admonition, the writer made it clear, should serve to remind us that what Abraham did, in looking beyond the earthly blessing and onto the heavenly, serves as a pattern for us. Like him, our ultimate joy and motivation for faith should be the promise of a heavenly inheritance as opposed to anything earthly. For Abraham, faith ultimately worked toward preparing him for his heavenly home. Faith motivated him to leave his homeland; it motivated him to look for the earthly land of promise; but it ultimately motivated him to look for his heavenly home.

Shifting a little from Abraham's motivation for faith, let us recall that faith is a tool which God provided for us to achieve His purposes. This suggests that even more important than what Abraham's motivation was is what God's motivation was in making faith available to us. God is working toward bringing us to the heavenly home, as it is written, "*. . . for He has prepared a city for them*" (Heb 11:16). In light of this, then, it would appear to be logical to conclude that God's ultimate purpose for making faith available to us is for faith to be used for the ultimate function of helping us prepare for the heavenly home that is already prepared for us. What was commendable about Abraham was the fact that he aligned himself with God's plan in rightly appropriating faith; but it should be understood that all along this was the ultimate purpose intended for faith by God and continues to be so to this day.

"*But without faith it is impossible to please Him . . .*" (Heb 11:6). This affirmation came following the report of Enoch's testimony of faith of being taken by God and escaping death. And not only was he taken, the writer reminds us; but even more importantly, before he was taken, he had the testimony that he pleased God. Then the writer brings it home by letting his readers know that the only reason why Enoch was able to please God and in doing so become eligible for God to take him, was because he had faith; for without faith, no one can please God. In support of what has been said thus far concerning the role of faith in preparing us for glory, therefore, the testimony of Enoch becomes both a model and a symbol for all who came after him. It reminds us that the purpose of faith is to serve as the means of enabling us to please God; so that even if it occurs after we die, He will one day take us to that place where He is, just as He took Enoch.

As we begin to appropriate this insight concerning the ultimate intended purpose for faith, it becomes important for us to understand the full scope of what Enoch did in becoming a model for us. This is imperative since in doing so it should help us overcome some uneasiness we might have. It is understandable that no matter how close one's walk is with the Lord, very few would admit living their lives thinking moment by moment about getting to the heavenly city. In fact, it appears that not even Jesus wants us to do that, for He said we should do business until He returns (Luke 19:13). We have important business to take care of in this life, which, by the way, will have impact on the life to be lived in the heavenly land. Indeed, it seems quite fine to desire to live for a long time precisely for the purpose of taking care of such business. Jesus Himself has commissioned us to do His work and we should focus on doing it. And what about our children and many others who depend on us; is it wrong to want to be around for them? I think not. Even Paul noted the dilemma within himself of desiring to go to be with Christ for his personal benefit while at the same time wanting to remain with those whom he served in the gospel for their benefit (Phil 1:21–24). As we attempt to resolve this quandary, I believe we can find Enoch's example to be the solution. While faith ultimately works toward preparing us for glory, the precursor to that ultimate end, as exemplified in Enoch, is the object on which we focus our energy now, which is pleasing God. This is the equivalent of being heavenly minded.

As we recall in chapter 2, unlike Elijah who was aware that he would be taken, we are not told of Enoch having any such foreknowledge. His concentration was on walking closely with his God and fully pleasing Him. In doing so, Enoch evidently did what God expected of him; and in the process, he got far more than he could have anticipated. Likewise, we should not walk away from the discussion of this principle believing we need to think of our departure to heaven every second of the day. Again, to the extent that it can cause us to neglect the business at hand, which He has mapped out for us to perform in this life, it does not appear that God Himself expects us to do that. What is required of us now, which we can say is the equivalent of having a heavenly perspective while being on earth, is that we please God. By pleasing God, we literally have the best of both worlds: fulfilling our earthly calling of living righteously and carrying out the mission God called us to perform—which in turn prepares us for the second, that is, securing our heavenly abode for the occasion when our time on earth has ended. Thus in fulfilling the earthly vocation of pleasing God, the ultimate purpose of faith is automatically and simultaneously realized in our lives. By pleasing God, faith is able to accomplish its ultimate work of preparing us for our heavenly home.

ASSURANCE OF THE PROMISES

As we work toward a renewed understanding of faith, a major hurdle is overcoming some of our misunderstanding about the promises of God. We know that the word of God contains numerous promises. Our responsibility, as we lay hold of these promises, is to recognize several factors that surround them. These include understanding their context, such as if they were meant for a specific people in a specific period; knowing what their timelines are and if they have expired or even begun; knowing whether there are conditions attached to them or if they are unconditional, and the like. Unger outlines four categories of promises in Scripture in terms of to whom they relate: to the Messiah, to the church, to the Gentiles, and to Israel as a nation.[1] Familiarizing oneself with these categories and knowing where one's place is within them will play a major role in whether or not we interpret the promises correctly. For example, Psalm 2:8 speaks of asking of the Lord and He will give the nations and the ends of the earth for a possession. To avoid misinterpreting this Psalm and expecting to inherit what was not meant for us to inherit, one has to realize to whom the promise was directed; and it is clear from the context of the Psalm that the Messiah was the intended recipient of the promise. This example emphasizes the point that if we expect to know which category of people is being referred to when learning about a particular promise, as well as other dynamics surrounding it; we have to be conscientious students of the word of God, as was discussed in chapter 1. This being said, the importance of carefully studying the promises cannot be overstated, as it can lead to great harm in a life when someone develops false hope, only to realize that such hope was based on a misunderstanding of a promise in the word of God. Also, teachers of the word of God must be responsible to teach truth, and students must not be so careless or at times so gullible as to embrace hastily erroneous teaching because it excites. Instead, we should follow the example of the Bereans who went and investigated whether the things they had heard were true (Acts 17:11).

---

1. Unger, *Bible Dictionary*, 1039.

Understanding the promises contained in the word of God is necessary for the present discussion because in presenting faith as being ultimately intended to prepare us for glory, it may appear that such assertion would mean it is vain to hope for those promises that appear only to benefit us while we are in the earthly realm but have no merit for glory. On the contrary, that is not the message I intend to give. Every promise God makes us is ours, and we should trust Him by faith for each. Still, I contend that based on this renewed understanding of faith, one must be careful to study diligently to understand the factors that surround the promises. Before believing God for a promise, it is important to know whether it is available for us or not. Of course the relevance for knowing this is not for seeking a guarantee of the sureness of the promise, since every promise of God is sure (2 Cor 1:20). Conversely, it is for our well-being so that while journeying to glory, we can keep our focus on that target—glory—and not become sidetracked in becoming overtaken and consumed with worry or anxiety over the promises, especially when we do not see them coming to pass in our lives. Being clear on which ones are ours or not will eliminate much worry and anxiety; because in doing so, we will be content to do without those that are not intended for us, and we will be confident to wait patiently for those that are.

So while the promises of God are good, a false view of them can be harmful. On the other hand, when we are assured of them, we avoid being distracted from our ultimate goal as we keep our eyes fixed on it, *"looking unto Jesus, the author and finisher of our faith,"* as the writer of Hebrews puts it (Heb 12:2). Clearly, assurance of the promises was the main reason why the witnesses of the faith were able to continue the journey without taking their focus off the heavenly destination. As a matter of fact, the writer makes it clear, they saw the promises afar off and embraced them (Heb 11:13), meaning there was no need for them to fret over them. Although they died without receiving them, they remained assured of them because they recognized the timeline of the promises. Certainly they were theirs, but some would ultimately be realized only through their descendants.

Understandably, to speak of only realizing a promise through a descendant might seem like a contradiction, but such is far from the case. Consider this: God repeatedly told Abraham over the course of two and a half decades that his descendants would be innumerable as the sand on the seashore and the stars of the heavens. But notice, Abraham only lived to see one of his descendants, namely, Isaac, as the promised seed. Does this mean that God's promise to Abraham was never fulfilled as far as Abraham himself was concerned, since he never saw the multitude with his own eyes? Absolutely not! Though Abraham himself did not see its ultimate fulfillment, he died having absolute assurance of it. He understood that he could not live long enough to see the promise fulfilled in terms of the multitude of descendants. Yet God allowed him to see the promised child through whom the multitudes would come. Likewise, similar scenarios were witnessed by other elders. The writer does not list them, but assumes the reader's familiarity with Scripture to be sufficient enough to know of them. For example, King David who did not see the first temple, which he desired to build for God, did see it from afar through his son, Solomon, whom he was able to advise of its plans. He did not see it with his own eyes; but in assisting in the plans, he was not only assured that there would be a temple, but he also knew what it would look like (1 Chronicles 28). A similar example was Moses who, though he was not able to enter the land of promise, was able to view it from a distance, which gave him confidence that his labor was not in vain (Deut 34:4). There are other numerous examples in the word of God.

Not only are there illustrations in the word of God concerning this, but there are also compelling examples in recent history as well. Consider the African slaves that were brought to the west and subsequently suffered unthinkable inhumane brutality. For many, their only hope for deliverance was to trust in the promises of God, as revealed in His word. Many attempted to secure freedom for themselves, but while making their attempt I believe they understood that such freedom was not the ultimate one they hoped for since running and hiding would still be necessary while in their "freed" state. Understanding the state of affairs of their time, I think it is safe to say that many of them understood that freedom in this life would ultimately be their children's but not theirs; still, they were also assured that true and complete freedom could not be denied them because they looked to receive it in the heavenly city. This fact was borne out in many of the lyrics of pain and hope in many of the Negro Spirituals that continue to inspire hope even to the present day, since in them we hear of departure from this world of pain and unto glory.[2] They were confident of this by virtue of the fact that they strove to please God. We

---

2. See, for instance, Willis, "Swing Low, Sweet Chariot," para. 3.

Faith ultimately works toward preparing us for our heavenly home

know that Civil Rights leader, Dr. Martin Luther King, Jr., understood this concept well also, because he testified of dreaming of a better day for his people when there would be racial harmony and equality; this was the promise.[3] Still, he was aware that this would not happen in his day as he made that point explicit by identifying with Moses as having gone to the mountaintop and being able to view the Promised Land. Though he himself would not be allowed to enter it, he was assured of the entry of his people, which was the ultimate fulfillment of the promise.[4] Now who would have thought of it then, but in 2008, America elected its first Black President; this is further evidence of that journey into the Promised Land, which Dr. King foresaw! Now I strongly doubt that there is a reasonable person today who would accuse the slaves, Dr. Martin Luther King Jr., or any of the other Civil Rights leaders of not laying hold of the promises simply because the liberty which they testified of embracing from the word of God was not experienced in their lifetime. Sometimes, as was seen in their cases, the promises of God unfold over a long time.

Another important point to consider: we must be careful to remember how easily our vision can become clouded as we reflect on the promises of God because of our "privileged" positions today. The gospel has a universal message. Whatever we preach in America, for example, we should also be able to preach in every other part of the world. Remember, Jesus commanded us to preach and teach the gospel throughout the world and to make disciples of all nations (Matt 28:19). Thus it should be obvious: we should say the same thing to everyone because we preach the same gospel. Yet much of the way the gospel that is preached in America today is not appropriate for many other parts of the world, because it is not applicable in those areas. If we take the message, which we preach in America, to some of the so-called third world nations of the world where poverty and all that accompanies it is the norm and not the exception, this "American" gospel would fall apart! How could this be? And what should the nature of the message be that we ought to preach to those people who have been suffering for generations under oppression, which is systemic and coming from others who are in power? To the first question, I propose that there obviously needs to be a more comprehensive approach to the word of God in order to discover that universal message. Little nuggets of

---

3. King, "Dream," para. 12.
4. King, "Promised Land," last para.

thoughts should not be taken out of context and be assumed to be universal, but the whole of Scripture must be considered when formulating our ideologies and so-called theologies.

In response to the second question, let us recall the apostles' determination when they set out to preach the gospel to then known world. The apostle Paul provides some insight in reciting the occasion of Barnabas and himself being sent to the Gentiles by the leaders of the church, Peter, James, and John. He said, "*. . . they gave me and Barnabas the right hand of fellowship, that we should go to the Gentiles and they to the circumcised. They desired only that we should remember the poor, the very thing which I also was eager to do*" (Gal 2:9b-10). Their example is for us to follow as we preach the gospel. Instead of being caught up in enjoying our blessings, we should remember the less fortunate to share our blessings, thereby providing relief. This is central to the gospel, and we see it from the earliest stages of the church (see, also, Acts 2:44–47). In reality, poverty and oppression are ever present human realities (see Mark 14:7). When the gospel is presented to those in this predicament, the gospel should not "bless" their poverty and be further oppressive—by making them feel bound or guilty because of their status—but it should be restorative, not only in word, but also in deed.

Also helpful for answering the second question, let us recall that it was God Himself who told Abraham there would be a set time for his descendants to be delivered from oppression in Egypt (Gen 15:13–16). The promise of God was sure, yet the reality was, in that it would take 400 years to be fulfilled, many would eventually die without seeing it. Likewise, many today, for one reason or another—often due to nothing under their control—will not themselves see the fulfillment of many of the promises, but their descendants will.

Not accepting this reality can and does frustrate many. As a result, instead of keeping our eyes on the final destination by virtue of pleasing God while journeying, we lose perspective and focus. This is partly what Jesus cautioned against when he warned against being consumed with worry over our earthly needs, as important as they are, saying, "*Therefore do not worry, saying, 'What shall we eat?' or 'What shall we drink?' or 'what shall we wear?'*" "*For after all these things the Gentiles seek. For your heavenly Father knows that you need all these things . . .*" (Matt 6:31–32). That last statement in the quotation seems to point to the root of the issue: perhaps we have forgotten that God already knows our needs and does not intend for us to be stressed over whether or not we will receive them. Whatever He has promised us will come to us, and we should be confident of that. All He expects of us, as Jesus continued to say, is that we *"seek first the kingdom of God and His righteousness, and all these things shall be added to you."* In other words, our focus should be on pleasing God; this is what our ancestors in the faith did, and it is also what we are called to do, and when we do so we should also have the assurance of receiving every promise that is due to us.

CAUTION AGAINST LUST

While journeying in our Christian walk, we need to remain sober and vigilant. In this respect, a primary area to focus on and guard against is the weakness of the flesh. The term "flesh" is used in a variety of ways in Scripture, such as of meat and human nature itself.[5] For the purpose of this discussion, the particular usage of interest is its designation as being the part of human nature "implying sinfulness, proneness to sin, the carnal nature, the seat of carnal appetites and desires, of sinful passions and affections whether physical or moral."[6] Throughout Scripture we are repeatedly warned to treat this entity of our human experience as being a formidable foe. Paul admonished those at Philippi not to place any confidence in it (Phil 3:3); Peter warned his readers to avoid fleshly lusts because they do battle against our souls (1 Pet 2:11); our Lord also spoke of the weakness of the flesh and how relying on it will cause us to fall into temptation (Matt 26:41); and there are numerous similar warnings throughout the word of God concerning this enemy of our souls. So as we continue to analyze our approach to the promises of God, I believe it is necessary to consider the role that the flesh is likely to play in such approach, especially because of the potential danger it presents in being capable of turning even the noblest of desires into lusts!

Sadly, even the promises of God, which were meant for our good and enjoyment, can be lusted for. In such cases, there is no longer a noble desire for the blessings for merely obtaining the necessities of life or for simply enjoying some overflow. Instead, there is an intense yearning for them to satisfy our fleshly lusts. One key problem with this, of course, is that lust can *never* be satisfied; consequently, no matter what amounts we

---

5. Zodhiates, *Word Study Dictionary*, 1280.
6. Ibid.

receive of the things we lust for, it only leads to additional yearning for more. Thus this becomes a case where the balance between striving to please God and having the correct approach to the promises proves very critical. If we are consumed with desire for the promises, it will lead to lust and in the process God will not be pleased; but if we seek to please God first, which faith enables us to do, and rest in Him while trusting Him to receive the promises, we shield ourselves from lusting. Furthermore, such rest and trust only comes if there is first an assurance of the promises, which in turn is solidified when we understand the factors that surround them, such as their timeline and intended recipients, as was discussed above.

The crux of the matter is this: in our Christian lives, we walk a very narrow road. I imagine shoulders on either side of that road as on a highway, and just at the edge of each shoulder is a precipice. The narrow road represents the way of pleasing God (Matt 7:13–14). The shoulders represent veering off the straight and narrow road and indulging in a mode of seeking to satisfy the flesh; meanwhile, the precipices on either side represent falling into sin. While on either shoulder we remain on the highway, but only barely, and so are at a greater risk of falling over the cliff and into sin than if we remain on the road. Accordingly, it is of great importance that we take inventory and ask ourselves where we are on this highway. Are we on the straight and narrow, or are we relaxing in the "comforts" of the flesh as we seek to satisfy its lusts? Consider the reality of how the work of Christ is clearly being neglected by most parishioners in the majority of churches today. Virtually everywhere, pastors are finding it to be increasingly more difficult to find willing volunteers to do the Lord's work than ever before. In fact, many have to be enticed into doing the work by offering them some sort of salary or stipend for their services. Today, apart from worshipping, the majority of parishioners in virtually every church do nothing in the service of the Lord besides "warming the pews"! And why is this? Is it because God only tends to call a remnant of the people in every church to do His work? Of course it would be absurd to believe that. But could it be that the majority of the people are relaxing on the shoulders of the highway and are "chasing after" the promises of God in an attempt to satisfy their fleshly lusts? Clearly there has to be an explanation for the pervasive apathy in the church toward the work of the ministry, and conceivably our lusting has something to do with it.

In light of this new dimension to the argument, there is an important distinction to be made between the perspectives of the poor and oppressed *versus* that of those who enjoy more comfortable lifestyles, concerning the promises of God. We recall that the perspective of the oppressed is generally one of maintaining their focus on heaven while the more "fortunate" tend to focus more on the immediate enjoyments of this life. Because of their sufferings, most would pity the oppressed, which is commendable. However, while most would not desire to be oppressed, if we are truly people of God and find ourselves in that condition, we should discover that there is a special privilege that will be available to us, which those who are "better off" typically envy. The reason is, when those in comfort take greater and greater liking to the enjoyments in life, there is great risk of relaxing and falling prey to the flesh, leading to a lust for more and more of these things. Again, the risk is irrespective of whether the enjoyments are relating to the promises or not; the flesh simply does not discriminate when it comes to lusting. On the other hand, those in oppressive states tend to be less focused on superfluity; they are content with the bare necessities. Also, in this state, because they have no one else to turn to, they tend more to look up to God for sustenance than the "well off," and in the process are more focused on pleasing God. Accordingly, they are more inclined than others to allow faith to have its intended ultimate effect in them, which is to prepare them for glory.

Is there a way for those who are in more privileged positions than the oppressed to enjoy the promises while striving to please God as first priority in their lives? This has to be the case, since, if God provided the promises for us to enjoy, He logically must have also made it possible for us to do so while continuing to please Him. To do so, I think there are at least three conditions that must be met in order to safeguard against lust as we enjoy the promises, with the first two being necessary to be in place even before the promises are received. The first is what we have already asserted: we must have the assurance of the promises. Being assured of them vastly minimizes the risk of indulging in intense yearning and preoccupation in pursuit of the promises, which leads to lusting. Why should we worry, fret, or have inordinate desire for that which is already ours, even if we have not yet received it? On the contrary, when we are assured of a thing, especially when we know we will receive it at the right time, not a second before or a second after we should, we can relax and patiently wait for it. This is obviously the type of assurance that the witnesses in the faith possessed. We are told that they were assured to the point that even while the promises were still afar off, they embraced them as if already in hand (Heb 11:13). Now if one embraces something, there is no longer the possibility of him thinking of that thing as not being his. God wants us to have this type of assurance of receiving everything He has determined to freely give us. Doing so will make it highly unlikely that we stray into lust.

The second safeguard to keep us from lusting for the promises is to learn to be content. In being content, we learn to be at ease in whatever state we find ourselves in. One of the reasons why many lust for what is already theirs is because of an insatiable desire for fulfillment in some area of their lives. Such intense longing might be for riches (1 Tim 6:9), success, or companionship, for example. The word of God is then consulted to find promises that speak to these desires, such as God's intent to rain showers of blessings upon us if we would just ask (e.g. Zech10:1), or to bless us to overflowing if we simply give Him what is His in the tithe (e.g. Mal 3:8–12). This we do without taking the time to understand all that the promises entail, such as the form in which the blessing might come, or the Lord's desire to take us through a time of molding that may unfold as a period of isolation leading us to total trust in God for even our daily bread. Disregarding anything less than immediate enjoyment of the promises, we focus our energies and passions on obtaining what God has already guaranteed. As we do so, this effort tends to exceed that energy exerted toward striving to please God, not only in the area of abstaining from sin, but also in our readiness to do the things He calls us to. Again, this may explain some of the indifference to the work of God in the churches today.

The problem of lusting for the promises is therefore not due to anything inherent in the promises themselves, since they are good; but when an individual allows his or her heart to be drawn away into evil desire, although the promises are good, if they are the object of evil desire, trouble results. The only posture the heart can assume to keep it from wandering into this direction of destruction is to be content. In the state of contentment, one is not likely to chase after desires of any kind in a lustful manner. Whether full or hungry, married or single, rich or poor, enjoying plenty or being in need, if we are content we are satisfied in trusting God to supply all of their needs—and even desires that are pleasing to God. This is precisely what the apostle Paul testified of learning as he experienced being full and also being in need and abandoned; yet he remained content (Phil 4:11–12, 19).

Now contentment is by no means to be confused with "settling" or having a lack of drive or ambition; but on the contrary, we can be content and yet aggressively pursue what God has set before us. Recall the parable of the talents to explore how God feels when we "settle" (Matt 25:14–30). The talents may be likened unto those investments which the Lord expects us to make in our lives for the kingdom. These require taking risks of various sorts, like being persecuted and suffering losses in our lives that ultimately are gains for the kingdom. So to do like the foolish servant who buried the talent and failed to invest it to reap a harvest for the Master is not to be identified with contentment in any form. Instead, the King expects us to be aggressive within the lines that He allows us to be aggressive in pursuit, not of desires that will steer us away from Him, but of those He sets before us to embrace for His glory.

So yes, we can, and should, aggressively pursue the things that God has ordained for us; this is by no means a sign of discontentment. Rather, discontentment arises within us when, instead of resting in God, trusting in Him for our needs, and only moving at His command, evil desire creeps in, causing our hearts to yearn for that which we hope will satisfy our fleshly cravings. Then no longer do we simply await the companion that the Lord has for us, for example, but we seek companionship for pleasure outside the lines of what God has ordained in marriage; riches likewise are longed for, not simply to supply need, or to help others, or to fund the kingdom, or for "small" comfort, but for sumptuous living that can potentially be a great distraction from what is more important, namely, pursuing God's plan and purpose for our lives. Being in the state of contentment protects us from these traps and snares; and while in the state of contentment, if blessings are bestowed upon us, our liking for them will in no way threaten our affection for the One who provides them.

The third defense mechanism which we must adopt to keep us from lusting, as we hope for the promises, is to follow the example of Rahab the harlot. Her example is to be unselfish upon receiving the promise. As we noted earlier, even before Rahab was assured of the promise of deliverance by the spies, she displayed an unselfish demeanor by asking that her entire family be allowed to join her as recipients of that blessing. Likewise, as we hope for the promises, we must be mindful of the risk of longing for them strictly for ourselves. Typically, when God blesses someone, and that person hoards those blessings at his or her doorsteps, requiring bigger barns to be built over and over again to house them, the opportunity to bless others is not considered. This is a sign of selfishness, revealing that the individual is really satisfying lustful pleasures.

So here again is another dimension to the reminder that Paul in the book of Acts gave the elders at Ephesus when he said *"it is more blessed to give than to receive"* (Acts 20:35). At face value, it might seem to be better to be on the receiving side of a blessing, but upon analyzing the dynamic of giving and receiving, it should be clear that in more ways than one, the opposite is far more rewarding. One of the reasons is that if we receive only, the risk of eventually perverting those blessings into lusts is quite strong. On the other hand, when we are unselfish and share our blessings with others, the risk diminishes. Lust may even vanish, because as we get into the habit of sharing, our eyes open more and more to seeing the needs of others, and we take the opportunity to be channels to bless them. Then, even more remarkably, as we prove ourselves to be such conduits before God, He entrusts us with more blessings so that we can bless many others. What a blessing to be used this way!

God truly wants us to enjoy everything He freely and richly bestows upon us (1 Tim 6:17). Still, as we journey the straight and narrow road, we must be vigilant in remembering the risks of straying onto the shoulders on either side of that road. With respect to the promises, this requires employing the three safeguards: being assured of the promises, learning to be content with what we already have, and being unselfish when we receive them. In doing these things, we minimize the risk of straying off the road and onto the shoulders, which will take us dangerously close to the cliffs on either side. I do believe it is God's desire that we become mature with respect to receiving His blessings. We should learn to enjoy them, but not lust for them. Those that are meant for us will come to us, so there is no need for lusting for them. And above all, we must learn to be content; this is the ultimate proof of maturity.

STRANGERS AND PILGRIMS

While the above measures to avoid lusting should help us maintain our focus with respect to the promises, what is even more effective in this regard, is to remember that, spiritually speaking, we are not residents on earth, but strangers and pilgrims. If we embrace this perspective, it will keep our center of attention on the heavenly as the goal of our faith. This is what kept the elders' eyes fixed upward. The writer of Hebrews emphasized this point by arguing that it was because of this perspective that our ancestors in the faith were able to be content in dwelling in tents as strangers in a foreign land (Heb 11:9). Tents symbolized the resolve not to build nesting places, but always to be on the move. For us also, that action is symbolic of how God expects us to conceptualize and treat our tenure on earth. God does not want us to get so comfortable down here that we strive to build our own empires on earth instead of building His kingdom.

Christ—our perfect role model for how to conduct ourselves in this life—epitomized what it means to be a pilgrim on earth. Though He was rich, He became poor for our sakes, that is, for the sake of the kingdom (2 Cor 8:9). Being God, He had all potential to enjoy all the riches one could ever imagine and to live more comfortably than any king that lived before Him or would come after Him. Yet He was willing to deny Himself such pleasure and to put the work of the kingdom before His personal gratification. On one occasion, after being told by a would-be follower that he was willing to follow Him wherever He went, Jesus testified that although He was the Son of Man, He had no place He could call home to rest His head (Matt 8:20). Jesus was challenging him to consider the full cost of discipleship, which included living as a sojourner on earth. While this does not mean we should not have homes, it does highlight the mindset of the faithful who know they are only passing through this world, not allowing anything to hinder their ability to reach their final destination.

As pilgrims, we must realize that our primary duty, while passing through this land, is to do the work of an ambassador to represent the country of our citizenship, that is, heaven, while in the foreign country (2 Cor 5:20; Phil 3:20). Ambassadors do not seek permanent dwellings, for they will soon need to move again. Likewise, we should not dig our foundations deep into this world, for in doing so we cheat ourselves of many of the rewards that await us in glory, concentrating too much on investing in the things of this life, which have no eternal value. This idea is supported by Jesus' warning that we should not invest in treasures here on earth, but in heavenly ones (Matt 6:19–21). Those which we make on earth we will lose because of the intrusion of various predators who break into our security barriers and steal them; but those made in heaven are protected from all predators. As such, we should not be resistant to allowing faith to do its complete work in us, for in the process, eternal treasures are being stored up in that fully protected vault on high, where neither thief nor robber can break into and steal.

Of course, in the process of journeying, God might choose to bless us with various blessings through faith; but since faith is working to prepare us for our heavenly home, those blessings will always compliment that preparation. They will not steer us away from that course by causing us to be comfortable as residents, instead of ready as pilgrims. In the final analysis, the litmus test for whether many of the things we call "blessings" are truly blessings or not is if, despite them, we are able to maintain our focus on heaven, with the evidence being that we are continually striving to please God. Evidently, the patriarchs had this testimony because we are told that Abraham left his country in search of his new home while taking great possessions with him (Gen12:5; 13:2). Those possessions were increased and passed down to his son, Isaac, and his grandson, Jacob. Yet despite having them, all three continued to dwell in tents, thereby continuing to consider themselves as being on a journey for a different home. Their blessings did not divert their affection from the heavenly to the earthly. This likewise must be our determination as pilgrims: no blessing that is meant to be enjoyed on earth, no matter how bountiful, will deter us from our ultimate destination in glory.

Not only are we pilgrims, but we are also strangers here on earth. Yes, we know this by the way the world treats us at times; but even apart from that treatment, we should consider ourselves to be strangers in this world and see the world's goods as being strange to us. This reality is even better understood when compared to similar situations on earth, such as what happens when we travel to foreign countries. In those places, we encounter customs and foods, which are strange to us because we are not familiar with them. Likewise, spiritually, the world's goods should be strange to us because we are neither its residents nor its citizens, and we should be unaccustomed to its goods. Also, we should resist enticement to lust for those things since we know they will not be allowed inside the gates of the holy city, just as various items are not allowed into our country of residence when we declare our goods upon entry after traveling to a foreign country. Also, we should not allow them to distract us from pleasing God because not only will they not be allowed inside the city, but they contribute absolutely nothing toward making us eligible for entering it or securing any rewards there. As a result, at the most, we can enjoy them, but we do so loosely to avoid any negative impact on the outcome in eternity. And if worldly goods prove to have negative impact, we should abstain from them altogether and be content.

A CONCLUDING THOUGHT

The writer of Hebrews concluded his thought on the pilgrimage of the elders by noting that *"God is not ashamed to be called their God, for He has prepared a city for them"* (Heb11:16). This statement might seem strange because it appears to imply that there are times when God might be ashamed to be called His children's God. Instead of favoring such an interpretation though, I think it is better to recognize that the writer apparently, by that statement, wanted to emphasize the extent to which God was proud to have been called their God; even to the extent of preparing a city for them to dwell in. Just consider, the God of the entire universe has taken the time to prepare a place for them; and all praises be to God, for we know He has done the same for us also (John 14:1-3)! And not only has He prepared a place for us, but He has provided the means for us whereby we can prepare ourselves for that place, which means is faith. Faith thus ultimately works towards preparing us for this place.

This dynamic of God preparing a place for us and our preparing ourselves for it, calls to mind the promise that God has prepared a great supper for His children (Rev19:9). In this world, if someone takes the time to host a banquet in our honor, at the very least, we should be expected to be gracious enough to take the time to prepare ourselves for it. This means we will take a shower or a bath, style our hair, don fine garments, and of course, show up on time. On the other hand, it would be ungrateful of us to complain about the requirements for preparation, considering the thoughtfulness and effort put forth by the host to provide us hospitality. Now if these requirements are reasonable for something like a banquet or a dinner, how much more for the marriage supper of the Lamb, to which we have all been invited? The preparations that have been made for us include: the suffering, humiliation, and death of the Son of God; His going to prepare a place for us in glory; and His providing the means whereby we can prepare ourselves for that great occasion—faith. In light of all of this, let us not permit anything to get in the way of our preparation, but instead allow faith to do its complete work in us to make ready a people for the Lord.

Faith is working toward preparing us for glory, but it will only be effective if we allow it to have opportunity to produce good fruit in us. These fruits, which may be summed up as every righteous act that pleases God, while they sometimes may not appear to benefit us in the present, are ultimately beneficial for glory because they fulfill the eventual goal of faith—to prepare us for heaven. Let us therefore keep our eyes focused on glory so that even when many of the comforts of this life become more and more appealing, if they prove to be stumbling blocks to our progress as we journey, we will, with all readiness, abstain from them. Furthermore, since the rewards in glory far outweigh any present satisfaction of the flesh, let us resolve not to allow anything to hinder faith from producing fruit in us for glory.

Principle Six

Faith is not nullified by anything, not even death, our last enemy

"By faith Abraham, when he was tested, offered up Isaac, and he who had received the promises offered up his only begotten son, of whom it was said, 'In Isaac your seed shall be called,' concluding that God was able to raise him up, even from the dead, from which he also received him in a figurative sense."

Heb 11:17–19

Why Abraham is called *"the father of all those who believe"* (Rom 4:11)? Here we are in the process of exploring nine principles of faith, and the central figure in four of them is Abraham. I suggest that this is by no means accidental. Instead, his examples of faith are set before us as a model to follow as we trust God for the impossible; and in my view, this last principle in which his heroism is depicted is, of all his demonstrations of faith, the one that most emphatically portrays the true caliber of a man of faith he was.

This principle provides hope in the midst of trouble. Faith gives us confidence for the things we hope for in God, as promised in His word. Yet despite what we know the word of God to decree, there are still times when, upon considering the situation in which we find ourselves, together with the obstacles presented there, we tend to allow what we see to shake our faith to the point that we no longer believe that God will, or, in some cases, can, bring about the necessary change in our circumstances. The example of Abraham's faith, which we will examine in this principle, lets us know that there is never such an instance, however. No matter what the situation looks like or the size of the obstacles we encounter, as long as God has promised, even if the situation appears to be dead or it has already died, faith will not be denied the opportunity to bring about the promise; for faith is not nullified by anything, not even death, our last enemy.

Previously in chapter 4, we visited this story in the life of father Abraham, where God tested him to see whether he would obey Him, even to do the terrible command of sacrificing his own son. Also of major significance was the fact that, not only was Isaac his son, but he was also the son of promise. In addition, we recall that Abraham believed God to give him this son, even when he knew it was impossible from a human standpoint. He trusted God to produce the seed through which the multitudes would come. Now we see him willing to sacrifice the seed before even one child was born to him. Although the writer of Genesis did not comment on the events as the writer of Hebrews did, in saying Abraham believed that God would raise Isaac from the dead, I am convinced that the commentary found in Hebrews is by no means a contrived addition to the story but that Abraham indeed believed this. Logically, if Abraham truly believed God that Isaac was the son of promise, by being willing to offer him up as a sacrifice before he was able to have children, Abraham must have believed that God would also raise him from the dead. Otherwise, we can say he never believed that Isaac was the one in the first place. But since we know that God knows all things, even the hearts of men, and God testified that Abraham believed Him, we know that Abraham indeed believed God that Isaac was the promised one. Accordingly, as we put these facts together, we must acknowledge the truth of the Hebrews writer's assertion that Abraham believed that God would raise up Isaac from the dead. Further, in exploring the deep implications of this truth, we remember that Abraham received the promise through faith; and now at the point when it seemed as if the promise was about to die, because faith could not fail, the fulfillment of the promise remained unthreatened because not only was faith able to bring about the promise, but also to sustain it.

In this truth, therefore, we should find hope for the things we trust God for and are confident that He has decreed them to happen, despite what our eyes might see that looks contrary. Nevertheless, it must be acknowledged that it can be challenging in this area, especially when our situations look like they are not only already dead, but even decaying. Still, as convincing as the evidence of decomposition might prove to be, even that is no match for faith! To support this truth, we may call to mind numerous examples in Scripture that let us know that there is simply *noth-*

ing that is beyond God's reach of being resurrected. The first that comes to mind is the story of Aaron's rod that budded in Numbers 17. Upon becoming weary of frequent complaints against Moses and Aaron, the Lord told Moses to take rods from the leaders of every household, which totaled twelve. He was to write the name of each head of household on his respective rod then place it in the tabernacle of meeting, and on the following day, the one whose rod blossomed would be the person of God's choosing. Among the rods was Aaron's, and his was the one that not only blossomed, but also yielded ripe almonds as a symbol to validate him as priest before God and Moses who had previously consecrated him for the office.

Now if God caused a dry piece of stick to come alive again to the extent that it produced ripe fruit, why should we doubt His ability to do the same by faith to fulfill His promises today? And what can we say about the story of the valley of dry bones in Ezekiel 37? This story has the necessary components to inspire hope that what seems lifeless can receive life again. Ezekiel was taken by the Spirit to a valley containing numerous bones of dead men. Upon arrival, not only was the prophet impressed by the number of bones, we are told, but also by their aridity, which made it apparent to him that the men had been dead for a very long time. The Lord then asked the prophet the hard question of whether he thought the bones could return to life. So cleverly, supposedly to mask his doubt, the prophet's response to the question was that (only) God Himself knew the answer. Then the Lord told him to do a "ridiculous" thing, one the likes of what we spoke of in chapter 3: to prophesy life to the bones. And after prophesying to them, the bones came together in order and received flesh and skin, but no breath. Finally, upon hearing a second prophesy, the bodies received breath and became an exceedingly great army.

This story introduces to us an important aspect of what God expects of us as He causes our faith to be effective even in the face of the greatest of challenges, even death. We are not to assume a passive role in the process as if we are bystanders; rather, God expects us to speak words of life to our situations. This is why Ezekiel was told to prophesy to the bones. Indeed, God was able to do all that was necessary to return the bones to life on His own, but God wanted the prophet to share in the effort. In the same way, we must practice speaking words of life, which are essentially God's words. God is not glorified when we speak words of doubt and death into our circumstances. The capability of causing death or life in our situations is in the power of the tongue, we are told (Prov 18:21). This suggests that our tongues might just be the reason for many of our failures! God has given us the words of life to confess, but as we look around us we sometimes become dismayed; and instead of being believers of the truth, we become believers of lies. This practice is deadly, because it can cause us to miss out on our blessings. Imagine what would have happened if Ezekiel had been overcome by doubt when he beheld the imagery of heaps upon heaps of very dry bones instead of trusting in God to prophesy as God told him to do to make them live again! Should we then have expected the end result to be the same? Of course God could have accomplished it another way, apart from the prophet's involvement; but it is certain that if it depended on Ezekiel's participation, the end result would not have been the same. Similarly, there are times when we are called to play a vital role to secure the desired outcome, which requires embracing words of life and confessing them; but when we fail to do so, we deny ourselves the promise.

An important decision must be made whenever we enter into moments of testing of our faith and we perceive the certainty of death in our circumstances. Like Ezekiel, we must learn to confess words of life as they proceed from the mouth of God. In fact, there will be times when our circumstances will not only appear to be dead, but death will indeed be evident for all to witness because of the smell of ensuing decomposition. The choice will then be ours to make whether we will validate, confirm, and affirm death—or infuse life into the situation by confessing what God decrees, like Ezekiel did. We must be fearless in prophesying life according to God's word, even when others around us try to convince us of the presence of death. This is what Jesus did when he approached the tomb of Lazarus and commanded the people to remove the stone that covered the doorway to the tomb (John 11:38–44). Martha tried to discourage Jesus by warning him that there would be a stench since Lazarus had already been dead for four days. Nevertheless, Jesus insisted and commanded him who was dead to come forth, which he did!

What is the common denominator in each of the above three resurrection stories? The word of God had already gone forth proclaiming life: it was God who told Moses that Aaron's rod would bud; it was God who told Ezekiel to prophesy life to the bones; it was Jesus, the Son of God, who had told Martha previously that Lazarus would live (John 11:23); and likewise, if God speaks life into our situations, though they might appear to be dead and decaying, they shall live. This truth takes us back to chapter 1 where we learned that faith must be based on the word of

God. If God decrees a thing, it will surely come to pass. As a result we are assured that faith will by no means be nullified by anything simply because it is not dependent on itself, but on the word of God, which cannot fail. Moreover, we know that even our last enemy—death—is no match because Jesus defeated it in the greatest resurrection story in history, in which He rose triumphantly from the dead. His was the greatest because whereas the others eventually died again because of the power of sin, Jesus, being God's anointed, sinless Son, cannot die again; death has no more power over Him. So now that Jesus overcame death, He has all power to return life to anyone and anything, including our circumstances, even if they have died like Aaron's rod, or might be decomposing like Lazarus was, or have already dried up like the bones in the valley, to which Ezekiel prophesied.

In light of such persuasive demonstration of victory over the greatest of obstacles and the encouragement this brings us, there should be a resurgence of hope in various areas of our lives where we know that God has made promises to us but hope has been lost because we have allowed what we see with our natural eyes to cloud our spiritual vision. At one point we believed God for the promise, but soon after, when circumstances looked grim, doubt crept in. What does that say about our faith if it tends to fluctuate based on the way things look? Are we not called to *"walk by faith, not by sight"?* (2 Cor 5:7). If we allow what we see to govern how we believe, then we are doing the opposite of what we were called to do, since we will then be said to practice walking and believing based on sight. No doubt this is why in large part God allows us to experience periods of droughts and apparent death in our circumstances despite promising blessings and success. It is "cheap" faith to say we believe when all things appear to be going in the right direction. As a result, God often tests us to show us how much we really believe—by allowing things to go in the opposite direction for a while, where it seems like they will spiral downhill, out of control, and into doom and destruction. Only then will it be determined what our faith is truly based on, whether on the word of God or on what we see.

Like Abraham, we must believe God for the impossible, even if it means hope will have to be raised from the dead. Nothing nullifies faith, but if we lose heart and fail to believe, the promise might just die and never be resurrected. Many of us have seen evidence where the promise seemed to be in jeopardy. We once believed the promise that we would one day further our education, for example, and began the journey toward achieving that goal. Then a stoppage later occurred in the process for one reason or another, and the interval has now been so long that we doubt we will ever see the fulfillment of the promise. So now that the promise appears to be as good as dead, we begin to speak a different language. Instead of talking about resuming the journey, we make plans for our future based on the current stage of education we have completed and any thought of advancing is eliminated from our minds. We once claimed that God promised the exact opposite, but now the question must be asked: "Did God say to further our education or not"? If the answer is yes, then no matter the reason for the pause or how long it was for, we must forge ahead! If God spoke it, it shall come to pass, and we can have faith to believe it, knowing that our faith will not be denied. The only thing that will prove successful in stopping us at this point is our failure to perform the works of faith, similar to those discussed in chapter 4, in re-enrolling in school, attending our classes, and applying ourselves to study. If we do these things, success is guaranteed by faith, because God's promises are sure.

There are also numerous other promises which we must continue to believe God for, though they appear to be dying. These include marriages that we know that God ordained, but they are now falling apart; the hope of improving various circumstances in our lives, although things seem to be going contrary; the hope of living long enough to accomplish more for the glory of God, although as we look at our health, hope seems to be fading. No matter the condition, we must focus our trust in the word of God and hold on to His promises. If God makes a promise, no matter how far beyond repair things might seem to be, it is never too late for God! Have you ever heard of marriages that have literally died by ending in divorce, yet God was able to resurrect them so that couples were able to reunite in holy matrimony then continued until only death caused separation? God can do it just for the one whom He promised a happy marriage to but there occurred a period of separation or even divorce in the marriage. And what about others who were given the sentence of death by more than one doctor, yet God proved who had the last word by allowing them to outlive their doctors? God can do anything He pleases to do; and if He has to raise someone from the dead to cause a promise to remain in effect, He will do just that. Abraham was "foolish" enough to believe God to raise His son from the dead so that the promise would be sure; and we must likewise be "ridiculous" in our faith to believe God to do whatever it takes to bring to pass the promises He makes to us.

Jesus taught that faith, even if only as small as a mustard seed, is sufficient to move mountains (Matt17:20). Mountains are perhaps the most awesome of all structures—natural or manmade—on earth. They are beautiful and graceful because of their sheer size and height. Yet it is this magnitude of an obstacle which Jesus claimed that faith will uproot from its foundation and transplant if the word of God decrees that it should be so. Accordingly, faith has the power to remove any size obstacle in order to bring to pass the word of God. Upon knowing this, one is not fazed by the challenges that seem to stand in the way of the promises of God. If we believe, they shall be moved.

Following his commentary that Abraham believed God to raise Isaac from the dead, the writer of Hebrews added the reminder that, figuratively, it was from the dead that Abraham had received him in the first place, so that the idea of raising him from the dead was not inconceivable to Abraham (Heb 11:19). This point is very important to emphasize since it represents the root of the problem of why we become easily dismayed and tend to give up on the promise when we see signs of death. We forget that we have nothing to do with the promise to make it a reality—absolutely nothing; indeed, not even the thought of it originated with us! It was God who planted the thought of the promise into our hearts to begin with. Looking back at Abraham, we recall that the promise came from the dead in that Isaac was conceived by Abraham and Sarah at the time when their reproductive systems were believed to be dead, from a biological point of view. On another level also, as we read the story of Abraham, it should be quite clear to us that even the idea of obtaining seed and the inheritance of the land came from God who called him from his homeland and introduced him to the plans of making him a father of a multitude and the inheritor of the Promised Land. No rational person is expected to argue that Abraham conjured up the ideas on his own. In the same way, the promises that God gave us became known to us only because God introduced them to us; and because of this, we can surmise, figuratively, that they came from the dead, bearing in mind that the ideas themselves were dead to us prior to God speaking them into our spirits.

Amazingly, we seem to find it easy to believe God for the things which He speaks into our hearts when He initially reveals them to us, even though they were previously not considered; but when we begin to analyze the possibility of obtaining them and to assess the obstacles that will need to be overcome to do so, doubt begins to set in. Thankfully, it is at this point in the process that the example of Abraham becomes most valuable as a paradigm for us. Just as Abraham was able to believe God to the point that not even death, the greatest of all potential obstacles, could stand in the way of his faith because he had previously witnessed God defeat this foe on two levels—the concept level and the physical birthing level—we must also persist in our faith to believe God for the "impossible" in the face of any obstacle, even the one where the death of the promise seems imminent! Whether we are at the point where we have seen evidence of the promise coming to fruition, or if it is still at the concept level, it makes no difference, we must not doubt and give up trusting God to see it come to pass.

Nothing, not even death, our last enemy, can nullify faith when we believe God for what He declares to us. It is hard to imagine that there is even one person who would refuse to honestly admit to allowing some dreams and visions which God has birthed inside him or her to die. Some dreams and visions, because they died at the concept level, were not given the opportunity to begin to come into being. Still others were given that chance, but when we saw the billows surround and threaten to overwhelm them from every side, we doubted and caused them to cease to exist from that point forward. Having now understood the truth that faith in God will conquer any enemy of the dream, this pattern of failure should come to an end in our lives. Let us therefore trust God and also thank Him in advance for bringing the dream to pass. We should have confidence to do this, knowing that as long as God has promised, the fulfillment is sure; for from the point of declaration on, nothing is able to hinder it from coming to pass. Faith is the key that unlocks the promise; and if we apply it, we will not be denied, because nothing, not even death, our last enemy, can stop it.

Principle Seven

Faith gives a voice to the dead

"By faith Isaac blessed Jacob and Esau concerning things to come. By faith Jacob, when he was dying, blessed each of the sons of Joseph, and worshipped, leaning on the top of his staff. By faith Joseph, when he was dying, made mention of the departure of the children of Israel, and gave instructions concerning his bones."

Heb 11:20–22

As I mentioned in the introduction, the inspiration to write this book came as a result of a sermon I had preached on these principles. At the time of preparing and delivering the sermon, there were nine principles, just as I believe the Lord revealed them to me. Upon writing, however, I considered combining the previous principle with the present one because of the similarity of the concepts to which they speak, as we shall see. Nevertheless, as I pondered and thought about doing so, the original structure prevailed—not only because that was the way it was originally revealed to me, although that consideration played a major role in the outcome, but also because I thought it would be helpful for the reader to study them separately since this seventh principle needs to be heard in its own right.

In the last chapter we noted that faith is not nullified by anything, including death. It thus follows that the voices of those who have spoken and those who continue to speak by faith do not die, but remain until those things which they declare come to pass. Under the present principle we will take a close look at the dynamic of how the voices of the fathers in the faith continued to speak long after their time to later generations that walked in obedience to their decrees. It is my hope that by taking this journey we will find encouragement to decree boldly the inner utterances which the Holy Spirit imparts to our hearts. In doing so, we will obtain the confidence to know that they will continue to speak to our descendants and future generations long after we have died.

It is interesting to note that among all of the heroics recorded in the roll call of faith—heroics such as walking with God so closely that God would consider to translate into heaven a person so that he would not see death; and of giving birth when biologically speaking it was well past the stage of being able to do so—there should be found the act of "simply" speaking blessings upon one's children concerning future things. This is what Isaac and Jacob are said to have done, and apparently the writer who compiled the roll call esteemed this act as being on the same level with those other actions which many would consider to be far greater. The reason of course is simple: it required faith to do both the "little" things and the so-called great things; neither was dependant on the individual through whom they were performed. We are the ones who esteem one action as being greater than another, when in principle they are actually equal. Without faith, none of those actions would have been possible, which implies that none was greater than any other; they were all amazing alike and represented performing the impossible and the "ridiculous." Having this in view, the actions of faith by the patriarchs to speak about things that would later manifest in the lives of their descendants should be recognized as being on par with the other acts of heroism of the other witnesses.

Accordingly, this should encourage the "least" among us who do not consider ourselves to be in the league of the "greats." Though our acts of faith may not appear to be significant from a human perspective, to God they are just as important as what others have done. In God's economy, the sign of greatness is measured by one's obedience to do whatever He commands us to do. If, in obedience to God's command, we simply speak words of life by faith to our children concerning their future, it is just as great an act in God's eyes as the laying on of hands by faith on a lame person who walks immediately thereafter. It is essential for us to realize that God needs all of us to work in His field. No matter how "insignificant" the task, it is a necessary one, nonetheless. Without it, the entire crop is affected, and the yield will be less than it could have been.

This is exactly what the Apostle Paul spoke of when he condemned the idea that some in the body of Christ were considered to be more significant than others (1 Corinthians 12). Using the analogy of the human body, he categorically denied the legitimacy of such claims by pointing out how important even the smallest and seemingly insignificant parts of the body are. I can personally testify to the truth of that argument because of a recent experience. One morning while walking into my bedroom, I accidentally kicked the door with my left small toe and fractured it. For the next few weeks I learned experientially just how important that tiny part of my body is. In walking, I found myself compensating for the loss of full function of that member of my body. I so compensated that my left knee began to hurt when I walked! Oh how important that little member is!

Each of the roles we perform in the kingdom is similarly important, though we often fail to realize this in certain areas, such as in speaking words of life by faith to our children. To emphasize just how important this role in the kingdom is, think of the fact that as great as the tribe of Judah was in being the one through which the Messiah should come, it all started with Judah's father, Jacob, telling him of these things centuries earlier (Gen 49:8–12). Likewise, every one of the "greats" in scripture had parents; and although the roles of those parents are not largely recorded for us to learn of, the fact that many of them played a major role in their children's accomplishments by speaking to them and teaching them the ways of the Lord, is undeniable. We are told of the role of Samson's parents in his life (Judges 13); of Samuel's mother, Hannah, (1Sam1—2:11); and of John the Baptist's and our Lord's earthly parents (Luke 1-2). And let us not forget the likely roles of the parents of many others, such as the parents of the prophets and the apostles, but concerning which there is no written record. Though all may not have had parents that played a role in their faith, it is doubtless that many did. Which role was more important, that of the parent who spoke into the life of the child and nurtured him or her in the ways of the Lord, or the child's who performed the "heroics"? Neither was greater, since they were both done by faith.

It is thus imperative that we practice speaking words of life by faith to our children; and just how important it is to do so is incalculable. After we have died, they will still hear those words. I remember the role which my grandparents—especially my grandmother—played in instilling godliness in my brothers and me when we were growing up. Not only did she ensure that we were exposed to godly influences by taking us to church and endeavoring to foster a Christian environment in the home, but to this day I can still hear many of the words which she spoke to us concerning the things of God and our responsibility to attend to them. My grandmother eventually went home to be with the Lord just over a year before I gave my heart to the Lord, but played a key role in leading me to Christ. She was not favored to see the fruit of her labor in this respect, yet her example and words of life which she spoke by faith continued to live on long enough to cause that fruit to come into being. In sincere honor and appreciation of the example that she was in my life, therefore, at my ordination, I was compelled to make mention of her; and it is with great pleasure that I make mention of her in this book also, because without her influence, this book might not have been possible. Even at this very moment as I write, I shed tears as I thank God for her. Her voice still lives on by faith and continues to be heard; not only by me and those who knew her, but also by many others who did not know her, because they are able to hear it through me!

Similar stories can no doubt be told by many others today as they continue to hear the voices of those who have preceded them in death. We can do the same for our children and others whom we will one day leave behind in an uncertain world. It is one thing to know something on the inside, but to declare it does wonders to the hearer! There will be times when our words will be needed to caution, encourage, and affirm many after we are gone; but if we refrain from proclaiming them now, they will not hear them then. Those words may not always sound like joyful music to the ears, however. In fact, as we look at the words of Jacob, which he spoke to his sons in Genesis 49, we find that such was far from the case. His charge to Reuben, Simeon, and Levi, for example, being the first words which he uttered, did not sound like words which those children may have been pleased to hear. The same may also be said of Esau following Isaac's pronouncement of blessings to him; as a matter of fact, because of those words, Esau hated Jacob and vowed to kill him after their father's death (Gen 27:38–41). So the word might not be flattering; but a flattering word might not be what will be needed in the future. In addition, the word might also be conditional, in that there will be blessings for obedience and discipline for disobedience. But irrespective of the nature of a word, we are called to speak it to our children now so that they will hear it perpetually, and even pass it on to future generations.

SPEAKING THE PROPHETIC

Speaking of things to come is not only a matter of declaring blessings to our children, but this action is only one aspect of something much larger.

That larger concept is the speaking forth of the prophetic. This truth is borne out by the inclusion of Joseph's proclamation among those of Isaac and Jacob. Whereas Isaac and Jacob addressed their immediate descendants, Joseph spoke of things that were much larger in scope concerning the Israelites as a people and their responsibility to give his remains a proper burial in the land of promise, although they were initially buried in Egypt. While it is unquestionable that the words of Isaac and Jacob, which they spoke to their children, fall under the umbrella of the prophetic, Joseph's words call this truth more to mind. When we think of speaking of future things that concern our children in their hearing, the prophetic nature of such utterances may not readily come to mind, perhaps because we consider such action to be only parental. Nonetheless, it is prophetic, and we should not refrain from performing it.

Joseph's example emphasizes the prophetic ability which faith gives rise to. It was just before his death that Joseph uttered words that would require a long 400 years to be fulfilled! He spoke of the Israelites' deliverance from bondage in Egypt and their exodus to the land of promise, which God had sworn to Abraham, Isaac, and to Jacob, that they would receive as an inheritance. He also gave instructions about taking his bones in the exodus to be buried in that land. Just as his father and grandfather had done before him, Joseph, in full assurance by faith, prophesied about things which would happen long after he was dead. And not only was the time factor impressive, but also the fact that he did so without seeing any evidence in advance that pointed to the possibility of such things coming to pass. This is a far cry from so much of what is said to be called prophecy today. Many today proclaim so-called prophecies concerning various issues only because they themselves have some level of control over the outcome; and with that, are confident to step out and predict it. A prediction is therefore made then great effort is put forth toward making it come to pass. In truth however, if such are the grounds for making a prediction, then any such so-called prediction should not be considered as prophecy, which is only through faith, as the patriarchs demonstrated.

In comparison to Joseph's prophecy also, many of today's "prophecies" are only uttered when the signs are convincing enough that what is hoped for will be inevitable. When this is the case, if the prediction is truly a prophecy, we can say it is safe at best. This is so because as the apostle Paul says, "... *hope that is seen is not hope; for why does one still hope for what he sees?*" (Rom 8:24). So to wait until there is no longer a need to hope negates the predictive aspect of a word; at this point, it may be classified as speaking forth what is already evident. In addition, we must remember that it is faith, not sight, which *"is the substance of things hoped for"* (Heb 11:1); so that once there is visual confirmation of one's hope coming to pass, even if the matter is of God, to declare it at this point would go beyond the realm of speaking a safe prophecy in terms of speaking of future things, but cross into the sphere of simply stating obvious fact. Faith gives us the assurance to speak in advance of seeing the manifestation of the things promised to us by God; and since we have this assurance, we also have the authority to speak them into existence, since they are sure to take place.

This assurance by faith allows us to declare truths not only at the time when we do not see the signs of their fulfillment; but even more impressively, we can also do so when all indications point in the direction of our hopes never becoming a reality. With regard to speaking prophetically to our children, perhaps there is someone presently reading this book who knows exactly what I mean. The Lord has placed a word in your heart concerning your child, but the more you believe, the worse that child behaves. Or maybe someone has the feeling on the inside; and even more than a feeling, but the assurance of the word of God by faith that all is well financially, yet things continue to get worse as the threats to cut off services and even to evict are mounting. God has given someone else the guarantee of his or her marriage being joyous and long lasting until death; yet all signs, instead of pointing in that direction, point to the speedy death of the marriage. Nonetheless, in each of these cases and countless others, because the word of God has gone forth and has been received by faith, words of life must be prophesied. Remember, since *"we walk by faith, not by sight"* (2 Cor 5:7), we have the assurance of the things which God has promised, so we should prophesy them.

In the previous chapter, we were comforted to know that we can believe God for His promises since nothing, not even death, can prevent faith from bringing them to pass. At this point, the word of comfort is to be bold enough not only to believe this, but also to prophesy it! This becomes necessary especially when others need that assurance of faith. A compelling example of why it is so important to do this may be noted in the story of the shipwreck which the apostle Paul and many others suffered while on their way to Rome to stand trial (Acts 27). Paul's advice to the centurion not to continue sailing from a place called Fair Havens due to his perception that the trip would end in disaster was ignored; and just as he predicted, they encountered a violent storm. Then came the chilling admittance of everyone on board, *"now when neither sun nor stars appeared for many days, and no small tempest beat on us, all hope that we would be saved was finally given up"* (Acts 27:20). But after many days of fasting and apparently when God had allowed the situation to get to its worst, an angel of the Lord appeared to Paul assuring him that no lives would be lost, only the ship. Paul in turn was not reluctant to declare this message to everyone else on board—but comforted them that they needed not to be afraid, because all would survive. He did so at the point when it seemed clear that death was imminent. Surely he could have kept it to himself, but his secret knowledge would have done absolutely nothing to comfort the rest who were terrified of the inevitability of death overtaking them. Likewise, let us not keep the word to ourselves, unless, of course, God commands that we should, but declare it, because it can bring comfort to the fainthearted. The same must also be done even if we realize that the things we will declare can only take place after our death; for even after we are gone, those words will continue to give comfort, because they are sure.

Thus, to step out on faith, to speak of things to come, as the patriarchs did, should be seen as the "greatest" of leaps of faith, because we may not be given the opportunity to see those things come to pass. The believer can depart this life without ever seeing his/her prophesies come to pass, yet he/she departs with full assurance that they will. Of course, this assurance only finds its dependence on the fact of the first principle of faith being in effect, which is faith being based on the word of God. As such, the patriarchs were not able to speak in confidence on their own accord concerning future things; rather, they pronounced the blessings which God Himself gave them authority to speak. As a result, their words of blessings spoken to their children were actually God's words, which could not fail. They spoke by faith according to the word of God; so that although they knew they would not live to see those things come to pass, they also understood that they did not have to because the fulfillment of those things did not depend on them, but on the authority of the word of God. Accordingly, though they were dead, their utterances did not die—because their words, in that they were really God's words, remained alive and in effect. The same is true for everyone who speaks the word of God by faith: their voices will extend well beyond their lifetime and will continue until the time when the things which they have decreed come to pass; so that faith does indeed give a voice to the dead.

Especially with regard to our children, our children's children, and so on, just as it was in the case of Isaac and Jacob, this truth is of special importance to us. Again, many of us tend to focus on the "great" acts of faith and strive to do them; and while there might not be anything inherently wrong with having such ambition, we must be careful in the process not to neglect this equally "great" right of ours. Once God reveals truths to our hearts concerning our children, we must step out on faith and perform the works of faith, which we discussed in chapter 4, and speak forth those things to our children, instead of safely keeping them in our hearts. In doing so, we must also confess to them that although we may not live to see those things unfold in their lives, we remain confident that they will nonetheless, because the mouth of the Lord has spoken them into our spirits. Our children's future does not only depend on our belief in the promises of God, but also, in many cases, on our proclamation of those things in their hearing. Also, we must remember that while it is important to believe, it is likewise necessary to keep in mind that faith without works is dead. If we fail to speak when God commands us to, then the word that must be spoken in order to be fulfilled will not come to pass. Despite our "believing," our failure to do the necessary accompanying works will cause our faith to be incomplete and therefore ineffective. Why else did the prophets proclaim the word of the Lord—other than because God wanted it to be heard? Similarly, often we are required not only to believe the word of God, but also to declare it. Let us do this, then, knowing that even if it is after our death, many will continue to hear our voices. Our voices will continue to declare the word of the Lord to the intended recipients, because faith gives a voice to the dead.

Principle Eight

Faith sees beyond the present "pleasures" of this life

> *"By faith Moses, when he became of age, refused to be called the son of Pharaoh's daughter, choosing rather to suffer affliction with the people of God than to enjoy the passing pleasures of sin, esteeming the reproach of Christ greater riches than the treasures in Egypt; for he looked to the reward. By faith he forsook Egypt, not fearing the wrath of the king; for he endured as seeing Him who is invisible"*
>
> Heb 11:24–27

Fittingly, this next principle will prepare us for the climax of our journey through the principles. As we look at the amazing step of faith which Moses took, we should find encouragement to do likewise, as on a moment by moment basis we are called to deny ourselves this world's pleasures, as we endeavor more and more to walk in the Spirit.

As we reflect on the life and ministry of Moses, taking into consideration what seems to be emphasized most, there might be a tendency to focus more on the events that unfolded in his life from the time of his encounter with the Lord in the burning bush and continuing until his death. These events include his meetings with the Pharaoh, the pronouncing of the plagues, the crossing of the Red Sea, and the wilderness wanderings. But in the verses that were quoted above, the writer of Hebrews reminds us of a very important decision that Moses had to make before he could accomplish those heroics. This was a decision that if it was not made, none of those other things would have mattered or even occurred. This was the decision to refuse to continue enjoying the lifestyle of comfort and pleasure in Egypt in the king's palace, but to choose to identify himself with the people of God. In all likelihood, we are all aware of his choice; but just how remarkable a choice it was, we might not fully understand or appreciate, since we can never relate to his exact position. Nevertheless, there is enough in the record to help us catch at least a glimpse into Moses' world, and thereby obtain a high level of appreciation for his self-denial for the sake of the things of God.

During Moses' time, Egypt was a thriving nation that, because of its great power and wealth, was one that could provide great benefits for some of its citizens. Moses, therefore, because he was the son of the daughter of the king of this great nation, had the finest of everything. For example, he was given the best education, as Stephen noted (Acts 7:22). Moreover, as Biblical scholar, Leon Wood, suggests, he no doubt had opportunity to advance to a high level of governmental office in the Pharaoh's court.[1] All of this points to a life of prestige, comfort, power, and wealth, which Moses must have enjoyed. But such was also the way of life that he refused to continue to live when he chose to identify himself with the people of God. Lest we lose sight of how remarkable this decision was, let us recall that the people of God were enslaved in Egypt at the time of his decision, so there was nothing glamorous about their status to desire. In fact, it was as a result of this unglamorous status of theirs that he made his remarkable choice. On one occasion as he observed the plight of his people, he witnessed an Egyptian beating a Hebrew, and because he thought no one would know of it, he killed the Egyptian and buried him (Exod 2:11–12). Furthermore, when he made his decision, he had not yet encountered God at the burning bush nor had been told as yet about the deliverance of the Israelites from bondage. He may have been aware that it would eventually occur if he was familiar with God's promise to the patriarchs; but judging from the fact that the bondage had already gone on for centuries, it is questionable that he expected it to come in his time, and especially through him. Something profound must have impacted Moses therefore to explain his amazing resolve. That thing, the writer of Hebrews lets us know, was faith. Only faith could have caused Moses to make such a radical shift in his allegiance.

Only faith could have caused Moses to look beyond his life of ease and comfort and decide to identify himself with the people of God, who were being enslaved. It had to be faith since he was unaware of what was in store for him. He trusted that a life lived for God was far better than the treasures of Egypt. Though he had not yet witnessed anything other

---

1. Wood, *Israel's History*, 95.

Faith sees beyond the present "pleasures" of this life   103

than slavery in the life of the people of God, which could not have been desirable, he was determined not to continue to enjoy the comforts of the Pharaoh's court while his people suffered at the hands of the same court. His actions were commendable, because very few would have done the same. Moses' remarkable choice, therefore, should serve as the model today for the people of God with regard to the choice that each of us must make through faith, in forsaking the world for the sake of Christ.

MOSES, THE IDEAL MODEL

It is interesting that the writer of Hebrews asserts that Moses esteemed the reproach of Christ as being greater riches than what Egypt had to offer, although Moses lived centuries before Christ was born. As a possible explanation for this historical gap, it could be that in contemplating the resolve that Christians must make in terms of siding with Christ *versus* the world, the writer may have considered Moses' choice to be one which Christians should emulate as the ideal model, seeing we may face the same struggle. Thus in viewing our struggle as being the same as that of Moses, he, in effect, considered Moses' choice as being one of whether or not to follow Christ. Craddock notes that this commentary by the writer of the epistle is consistent with the theme he presents of looking beyond the present for the reward, as seen in the example of Abraham where he "looked beyond the land to the heavenly city."[2] So, in similar fashion to Abraham, Moses is presented as looking beyond any reward he could have received in his lifetime, and unto that which Christ had in store for him if he became His follower. Moses, the writer reminds his readers, made that choice; and it was an outstanding one, worthy of emulation. Indeed, it should be motivating for us today as it displays rejecting the world and its pleasures for the sake of Christ.

To this end, the writer laid out several key components of Moses' example for his readers, to which I believe we should pay close attention. If we do, we should be inspired to reproduce them as we engage in the fight by faith to choose the sufferings for Christ over the enjoyments of the world. At the outset, we understand that there was first a "coming of age" that Moses had to undergo before he was able to see the light to choose the greater riches. We are told that he made his choice to no longer consider himself to be the son of Pharaoh's daughter "*when he became of*

---

2. Craddock, "Hebrews", 141.

age" (Heb 11:24). While this "coming of age" may be seen as being strictly chronological—occurring at a set age in his life—since it is obvious that there had to be a set age when he made his decision, the deeper implications of "coming of age" should not be overlooked. Just as it is clear that he made his decision when at a particular age, it should be equally clear that such age was not marked on his calendar as a date when he should make the switch from identifying himself with the Egyptians to with the people of God. Rather, his "coming of age" must be understood as being a point of maturity that he reached when he ceased to see through the natural eyes only, but through the eyes of faith to understand that the present pleasures in this life are nothing to be compared to that which awaits those who follow God!

No matter one's chronological age, there is a point of maturity which has to be reached before being able to choose Christ over the world. This is the reason why many of us fail in the struggle to deny ourselves of the pleasures of this life that oppose the ways of the Lord! Many are chronologically old, but are yet to "come of age," because they are immature. The age of maturity comes at various points for different individuals. It commences with the conscious decision to surrender one's all for Christ, after which occurs a gradual increase to even higher levels of maturity through a process of prayer with fasting, meditating on the word of God, and fellowshipping with and being held accountable to other mature believers in Christ. Accordingly, this is by no means a one-time, once-for-all decision, but a process that continues throughout one's life. Only through this process are we able to make the difficult decision—and even more importantly, maintain the stance for Christ to suffer reproach for His name in denying ourselves of worldly pleasures.

Just as was the case for Moses, "coming of age" or maturity represents for us not only the initial step in the process of deciding to choose Christ over the pleasures of this world, but also how that decision will proceed over time. To clarify, once the initial decision has been made, then comes the follow through, which is equally as important as the initial decision, for if it is not adhered to thoroughly, the benefits of having made the original decision will be diminished or negated. To insure that this does not occur, the process of maturity must be allowed to continue in us. Maturity thus makes the difference—whether a decision will be made based on emotion alone, only to find a short time later that there is nothing left for the follow through, or, following the decision, one endures over time. Choosing to follow Christ is a decision of this sort because it requires significant sacrifices of the individual, and only the mature will be willing to make those sacrifices and endure. Moses demonstrated this level of maturity. He was aware of the implications of his choice, yet he was willing to follow through with it, because he was fully grown. Going on the side of God's people meant the acceptance of suffering and affliction. To Moses, this was apparent since he witnessed firsthand what the people of God suffered; but again, what he saw did not daunt him because he was determined to be identified with God's people.

Lack of maturity is why many do not make the admirable choice that Moses did. Moreover, when the decision is made and there is failure to maintain it, this reveals a misunderstanding of maturity as an on-going process. Over time, affliction and suffering will expose this immaturity. In Moses' case, the suffering was ever before him as a constant reminder of what to expect upon making his decision. He may have been aware of this early in life, but it was only when he became of age that he decided to identify with them. For us, it is unclear whether we are always aware of the sufferings and afflictions that accompany the decision to follow Christ. We hear about it and read about it in the experiences of many in Scripture, in the experiences of others in distant lands, and even of some who may live just across the street from us, but it is questionable whether we understand or accept the notion that it will come to us also. Many come to Christ, but unlike Moses, during the initial stage of the decision process they fail to understand that the sufferings and reproach for the name of Christ will follow. When it comes, the maturity or immaturity of each is exposed.

New Testament scholar, Virginia Wiles, gives helpful insight into why suffering and reproach is connected to the life of faith.[3] Classifying faith as "a suffering faith," Wiles argues that the life of faith often leads to suffering primarily because of two reasons. First, the follower of Christ faces conflict within because of the struggle between the old life and the new—because of the new commitment and the constant struggle to forsake old ways. This is suffering! Secondly, because the individual has made the decision to become a follower of Christ in a social context, those around him/her might not be supportive of the change. Friends and family might not like the new lifestyle, especially if it impacts the way they

---

3. Wiles, *Paul*, 130–132.

once related with the person. In fact, Wiles goes on to say that the new disciple of Christ might even be perceived as a troublemaker. This can lead to estrangement and even persecution, which, too, is suffering! A decision must therefore be made whether to endure or to surrender to one's inner struggles and/or society, or to persevere and faithfully follow Christ. The latter choice is one that only the mature will be willing to make.

In this sense Moses' example is again proven to be a model for us because there was nothing obscure to him about what he would face upon making his choice. Tragically, as opposed to what we see in his example, the road appears foggy to many who come to Christ, because suffering was not presented to them as a likely component of the new life. Those who bring others to a "Christ-without-suffering" do an injustice to the cause of Christ. In this country, the gospel is often presented as a life of prosperity and an absence of pain and suffering. This includes prospering financially, in health, in relationships, and in a multiplicity of other ways. What those who present the gospel this way fail to mention, however, is that such "ideals," especially in the area of finances, are usually only evident in the lives of very few. While some may simplify matters by calling their blessings the inheritance of the children of God and that all we need is faith in God to receive them, in truth, very few will ever see those blessings. Some are indeed blessed to see them for various reasons which others, for reasons that only God ultimately knows, will not enjoy. For example, some are leaders of large congregations and enjoy many benefits in that role; others are "celebrities" in the gospel, such as singers and evangelists who receive excellent compensation for their services; still others may have made good business ventures or have high paying jobs. In contrast, if we are to take an honest survey of the vast majority of the people of God, not only of today, but also from thousands of years ago, we will find that the average child of God did not and does not enjoy such comforts as they enjoy. Also, we are not always privy to all the happenings in the lives of this "elite" few; and if we were, we would realize that in some cases all that we see is not necessarily as it appears. Finally, some of what many claim to be blessings are not truly blessings at all, because God had nothing to do with their obtaining them.

Even if someone devotes his or her life to God wholeheartedly, there is no guarantee of a life of comfort, ease, or prosperity in this life. On the contrary, what is guaranteed is a life of reproach for the cause of Christ, just as Moses, Jesus, the apostles, and many followers of Christ experienced. Remember, the gospel is universal in scope, so if what many teach about how to obtain prosperity and ease in this life is true, then the strategy should work well in some places, such as in some of the countries in Africa, in Haiti, and in other parts of the world where poverty is systemic and seems to have no end in sight. A "prosperity gospel" will not work there, because it is not a balanced presentation of the gospel; what will work there is the truth of the sureness of reproach and sufferings of some kind to be endured by every follower of Christ.

I do not intend to paint the life of a Christian as grim, because it is not! God does indeed bless His children from time to time in immeasurable ways, including finances. However, there is no valid indication of this being a guarantee for every child of God to experience, which is why if we are to do justice to the gospel we should be responsible to present the entire range of the good news as did the apostle Paul for the elders at Ephesus, to whom he made it known that his mission was to declare the whole counsel of God to them (Acts 20:27). Indeed, Jesus Himself warned us that if we desire to live for Him we must deny ourselves and take up our crosses daily and follow Him (Luke 9:23). The cross represents a place of suffering and shame; and if the Master Himself said we must endure it, why should we refrain from teaching that aspect of the message, or attempt to cloud it? Experiencing reproach, then, is an integral part of the life of a Christian; but only the mature will be willing to suffer it.

Moses embodied this resolve, along with his understanding that the pleasures in Egypt were only fleeting. Now as simple and as straightforward as this might seem, this understanding was also another mark of his level of maturity. It is clear that maturity is needed to comprehend this because multitudes of Christ's followers do not seem to grasp it, which is a sign that they have not yet grown up in Him. As we struggle between aligning ourselves with Christ or the world, this is therefore another determining factor for how we will fare. It may seem elementary to ask Christians whether we understand the reality of the temporariness of the world's pleasures; but whether or not we acknowledge it, only if we are mature will we truly understand! Just consider, if this understanding were indeed simple and straightforward, why then is there such a struggle to abstain from that which we know to be temporary, while at the same time we display such a weak affinity for that which we know to be profitable both for now and for eternity? Hopefully, in stating the problem that way, the supposed straightforwardness of the fleeting nature of the things of the world will not appear to be so straightforward or elementary after all.

Understanding the temporary nature of the things of the world is a matter of maturity mainly because the ability to abstain from them does not come simply from the intellectual knowledge of their brevity, or most would be able to do so. Rather, this ability is a spiritual matter in which one gains greater and greater ability to do so by faith, which also increases with closeness of fellowship with the Lord. Note, for Moses, this ability was given to him the moment he decided to side with the people of God and to accept the reproach that would follow; but it also only developed in him with increased knowledge of God. This fact is evident from the wilderness wanderings during which time the Israelites frequently gave themselves over to various lusts; but no matter how intense those lusts became, even when Aaron succumbed, Moses stayed the course—because he continued to walk closer and closer with God. Now if we recall the discussion of Enoch's faith, we will remember that walking with the Lord is a matter of faith. It was ultimately by faith, therefore, that, in exchange for eternal riches, Moses was able to refuse the temporary things that Egypt had to offer. This is why the writer of Hebrews noted that it was by faith that he was able to abandon those things as opposed to attributing that resolve to any intellectual insight on Moses' part.

This understanding that only by becoming mature through faith can one obtain the strength to reject that which is clearly fleeting, should explain why many today in the body of Christ are not able to see beyond the "pleasures" of this life. Many cannot see beyond them because of a lack of maturity, which is ultimately due to a lack of faith, since faith gives rise to maturity. In failing to see beyond these "pleasures," the obvious alternative is to lust for them and to pursue them. Whether or not we are able to obtain them, the end result will be the same: a love for the world and a resulting estrangement from God. Notice that I put the word "pleasures" in quotations. The reason for doing this is also the reason why the end result of being enticed to lust for the things of the world will always be the same: these "pleasures" are never truly pleasures at all, but sin. To be clear, these so-called pleasures are not to be confused with the blessings of God which are meant for our enjoyment, but these are things that are displeasing in God's sight. Now just as the writer did not hesitate to designate the pleasures which Moses refused in Egypt as being sinful, we must not hesitate to do the same in speaking of the things of the world (see Heb 11:25).

In addition, John made it clear that all that is in the world is sinful, so we should not be confused about this fact (see 1John 2:15–17). The sobering reality is that if we lust for the sinful, it is equally damaging to the soul as if we are actually able to commit the sin itself (see Matt 5:27–28).

As our paradigm, there is one other important trait that Moses embodied and the writer of Hebrews highlighted. Moses was said not to have feared the wrath of the king of Egypt. Now as we read the account in Exodus, we see that in killing the Egyptian who was beating the Hebrew, Moses demonstrated much courage; but when he realized that the matter was known, he ran away from the presence of the king (Exod 2:11–15). As we compare that account to what we find in Hebrews, there would appear to be a discrepancy between the two accounts concerning the issue of whether Moses was courageous or not. In continuing in the Exodus account however, we find that it was the same Moses, who, after his encounter with God in the burning bush, returned to face the king and challenged him to his face to let God's people go. This transformation tells us that the better we get to know God and the closer we walk with Him, the more strength we receive by faith to reject the temporary pleasures of the world. But that is not the only thing we receive. Simultaneous with receiving strength to reject worldly pleasures, as we note when Moses returned to face the king, courage is also received. Moses now had the courage to counteract fear of anyone or anything that stood in the way of getting to know God better and walking closer and closer with Him! Both the temporary pleasures of this life and the fear of opposition have the same effect on our Christian walk: they work to hinder our progress in God. As God gives strength to fight one, therefore, He also provides it to fight the other. This dynamic was illustrated in the life of Moses.

This quality was also evident in the life of many others throughout Scripture. It was demonstrated by the prophet Elijah who, after receiving the threat of being killed by Jezebel after King Ahab besought her, ran for his life; but after being strengthened by God, Elijah was bold enough to later stand before King Ahab and prophesy Jezebel's horrible death (1 Kgs 19:1–4 ; 21:17–23). Such courage was also evident in Peter who, following his shameful denial of the Christ because of fear, upon being restored by Him, became a bold witness of the sufferings of Christ (see the denial—Matt 26:69–75; the restoration—John 21:15–19; and the bold witness—Acts chapters 3–12). And what else could explain the bold stance of Paul in being a willing agent of sufferings for Christ other than the closeness of his walk with his God (2 Cor 11:22–33)? Similar courage was also displayed by many others in Scripture, including Daniel and Stephen, and also by others in more recent history, such as Dr. Martin Luther King, Jr., and many other Civil Rights activists who boldly faced their oppressors. This courage was present in them because they endeavored to walk closely with God. Basically, there is a rule of thumb: if we expect to challenge our fears which stand in the way of our progress in God, we must draw closer and closer to Him, which can only happen through faith, then we will find that no matter how great the fear, because of our close proximity to the Lord, we will be able to conquer it.

This quality, just like the others that Moses displayed, comes only through faith because it is only by faith that we can endure as he did in *"seeing Him who is invisible"* (Heb 11:27). Note that it was by looking beyond the visible and unto the invisible, the writer explains, that Moses was able to conquer his fear of the king. He looked beyond the object of his fear and unto the invisible God in whose hands his life was held secure. He knew that no matter what might happen to him, it could only occur if the Keeper of his life allowed it, and not because his enemy willed it. Now since we cannot see the invisible God with the natural eyes, but only through the eyes of faith can we receive this courage, faith thus becomes the means by which we are able to find courage to withstand our fears. This is how Moses was able to face the king, and it is the same way that we will be able to face those "kings" that stand to oppose our effort to choose Christ over the world.

Such "kings" may be others who might threaten to persecute us the same way the Pharaoh threatened to persecute Moses. Indeed, many do not only threaten to persecute us, but they actually do so. Persecutions sometimes manifest in the form of ridicule and estrangement from family and friends for the sake of Christ. Even more severely for some, especially many in foreign countries, threat comes in the form of physical harm and even attempts at genocide. Still, no matter the form, it is ultimately an attempt to instill fear with the objective of causing separation from Christ and to create in us a greater love for the world. Just as He did for Moses, God has strength available for us to overcome these fears; but the reality is, although it is available, we must access it by faith, just as Moses did.

As was mentioned above, the decision to choose to follow Christ instead of the world is a multi-faceted one, and only the mature will be able to follow through with it. The act of boldly standing up against those who try to instill fear in us is one of those facets. Just as maturity or the "coming of age" was the quality that enabled Moses to decide to turn his back on fleeting pleasure, it again is the factor that enabled him to withstand his fear. Consequently, maturity—a byproduct of faith—is the framework through which every facet of the decision-making process to follow Christ must work. In summary, then, the example of Moses is a remarkable model for us to emulate in order to obtain the victory through faith leading unto maturity that causes us to see beyond the present "pleasures" of this life.

THE CALL TO RESPONSIBILITY

Considering these things, the richness of the rewards of faith should now be even more appealing to us than worldly "pleasures"—to which we are drawn because of a lack of faith. This increased level of awareness of the difference between being rich in faith and lacking in faith should cause us to be vigilant in seeking to strengthen our faith, so that it can lead to greater levels of maturity to empower us to maintain and increase our freedom from the things of this world. This admonishment is not to be taken lightly, especially when we think about the alternative. Many were able to say that initial "no" but somewhere along the line in tasting more and more of the world's pleasures, they became dissatisfied with just a taste and desired a meal, then the "no" to the world's pleasures changed into a "no" to Christ! Isn't it a great tragedy that many would consider trading in their salvation for the "joys" of this world? Even more tragic is the reality that for many this notion is not only a consideration but an experience because they have indeed forsaken Christ for this same reason. One of the saddest portions of Scripture, I believe, is recorded at the end of 2 Timothy where the abandonment of many is lamented (2 Tim 4:9–16). Included in the number of deserters was a man named Demas. That this man had deserted Paul was sad but even sadder is the fact that the reason why he did so was because he was said to have "*loved this present world*" (2 Tim 4:10). In other words, more heartbreaking than his abandonment of Paul, was the fact that he abandoned Christ in favor of a love for the world! Tragically, many today have also purposed to follow the example of Demas as opposed to that of Moses, and we must be careful not allow this to be said of us.

Of course, not to allow what was said of Demas to be said of us is not simply dependent on our determination in our own strength to prevent it from happening. Obviously, at one point Demas was determined to follow Christ, and he did. What is also clear as well is that at some point he must have let his guard down; he failed to do the things necessary that were to cause his faith to increase and thereby increase his level of maturity. The apostle Paul expressed his frustration and hurt over a tremendous problem which has "plagued" the kingdom of God for far too long. Again, it is easy to miss the deeper implications of what truly happened when Demas forsook him. To be sure, he abandoned the apostle, but he ultimately abandoned Christ; and with that abandonment of Christ, he also caused damage to kingdom progress! Paul was appealing to Timothy to come to his aid quickly, because there was a great void created in the effort of doing the work of the ministry, since many whom he counted on had abandoned him because of the pursuit of worldly pleasures.

Ultimately, then, our immaturity in not being able to resist worldly allurements ends up hurting not only us but the progress of the kingdom of God! I frequently remind congregants that for the most part God chose not to use heavenly beings to preach the gospel. We do understand that angels are able to and do engage in human affairs from time to time (Heb 13:2). Primarily, however, the gospel is preached by humans (Rom 10:14). Given this reality, what then should we expect the impact on the kingdom will be whenever we forsake the things of God in exchange for the pleasures of this world? Obviously, its cause will suffer; and presently it is suffering immensely! I think we know that we need God for every aspect of our existence, but it is questionable whether we are aware that God is sometimes seen to have needs and that those needs depend on us! One of those needs is that God has subjected much of the success of the spread of the good news of the kingdom to our readiness to go out to do the spreading. It is God's will that it be done; but in order for it to happen, we must be willing to participate with God in the effort and get it done. So sometimes we are content in sitting back and enjoying temporary and meaningless pleasures while we look to see if ministry will get done in some area, but fail to realize that in order for it to happen we must put our hands to the plough and with God's help make it happen.

A related question arises: Why does God sometimes withhold promotion from many of us? This issue plagues many of us, not only in our "secular" work, but also in ministry. (I put "secular" in quotations because everything we engage in should be opportunity for ministry.) At any rate, promotion is sometimes due to us, but it is withheld for some reason, and this leads to great frustration. We are confident of our being faithful in everything God entrusted us with, and indeed we may be, to the full extent to which any human being can be. We have also tried our hearts and found that our motives are where they should be; we do not seek promotion for the purpose of boasting about it, but we believe it is time for it, we are deserving of it, and we will give God the glory in the new position. While in each of these areas we may be justified in our frustration, in many cases the reason why our promotion might be withheld is because of our not being able to resist the allurements of the world.

Of course, we might argue that such things do not entice us. Still, who knows the heart better than God? God knows our hearts even better than we do. Because He is aware of this weakness in us, God sometimes does not allow us to get to certain levels since at such heights we are able to taste too much of the pleasures of this life; and because God knows we will not be able to enjoy them without allowing them to pull us away from fellowship with Him, at which point sin is able to creep in, for our own good, He does not allow us to get to those levels. As a result, this again is another area where being mature proves to be so important. Yes, maturity signifies our ability to say no to the things of the world; but a lack of it not only means we will not be able to say no to those things, but it can also cost us the promotions that God intends to bring our way. Often we do not see this aspect of the equation, which leads to frustration and a loss of patience; then instead of waiting on God to elevate us in the fullness of His time, we manufacture our own promotions, which is an endeavor that always leads to disaster.

Perhaps you are wondering why God has not elevated you in ministry as yet. Ministry involves any position where God places us so that we can be a witness for Him or can edify other believers, which includes our jobs, our schools, our neighborhoods, and the like. Let us focus for a moment on some of those areas that we tend to think of when we speak of ministry, such as the pastorate, gospel entertainment, and evangelism. Many of us have ministered faithfully in these areas for years, but we notice that there is no increase in opportunity, borders of influence, size of the ministry in the case of a church, and so on. Understanding that the reasons for this could be many, or very complex, or be undisclosed to us, I do not propose to provide an answer as to one's disappointment. Still, I would like to suggest to those of us who are in this situation that we take a look at whether we are mature enough to be trusted with some of the pleasures of this life that will be sure to come with increase in ministry, without allowing those things to cause us to stray from God.

Important to note is the fact that motive does not have to be a factor here, so that we can appeal to our motives to justify that we are ready for increase because our motives are pure in that we do not seek increase in order to satisfy any lust but only to glorify God. In some cases our motives may very well be pure but God knows that when we get to another level we will not sustain or improve our relationship with Him. Why? We may not have been fortified enough in our spirits to handle what lies ahead. Many who had pure motives when God began to elevate them increased at a faster rate than they matured, and when they got a taste of some of the finer things in life, they strayed from God. This is expressly why the apostle Paul, in charging Timothy about the qualifications of those who should serve in leadership, warned him that a bishop, among other things, must not be a lover of money or be a new believer (1 Tim 3:3, 6). A new convert is immature concerning the things of God and must first be seasoned before being given such responsibilities as would increase opportunities for enticement for the things of the world. His motive may be good but the strength to withstand those temptations might be absent, as Jesus said, "... *The spirit indeed is willing, but the flesh is weak*" (Matt 26:41).

As a result, barring other reasons, God perhaps is keeping many of us at the level where we are for as long as He has because He knows what will happen as soon as we move up. The ministry thus stays at the number it has been at for several years; we have not yet obtained the contract with a major recording label for our album as yet; we do not receive speaking engagements in the larger settings as yet—all because God has decided not to allow it, because He knows that such "successes" will be detrimental to the relationship which we now enjoy with Him while we are at our current level in ministry. While God sometimes does this, the fact still remains that unless it is a case where He does not intend to expand our ministry but intends for us to remain where we are, understand that He is not pleased to keep us where we are but He does so for our good. God, in His forbearance, is waiting for us to grow up in Him so that He can do new and better things in us!

Instead of being frustrated over our stagnant positions in the work, then, let us channel that energy toward continuing to be faithful over the little entrusted to us by God and in drawing closer to Him. In doing so, our faith increases, which in turn produces maturity, which in turn enables us to say no to the allurements of the world, so that God can elevate us. It is essential that we grow up! It is one thing that our advancement in ministry depends on it to a large extent; but if that were all that was at stake, we might be able to live with it. More important is the fact that the cause of God depends on it! The reality that God's will is hindered and stifled because of our immaturity should cause us to sober up and attend to this matter! Imagine what would have happened if Moses failed to come of age but continued instead to enjoy living in the palace of the king? Because God had already sworn to Abraham that He would deliver His people, surely deliverance would still come, but the story would have been told differently because Moses might not have been the one through whom that deliverance would come. In reality, I am convinced, many stories that God intends to be told one way are being told another way because God has to improvise in many situations due to our failure to come of age so that He can use us in the way He intends to. Considering this problem, our resolve must be to do those things that ensure our continual growth in God, so that His purpose will not be thwarted because of us—but be advanced, because we are found to be suitable vessels to do His bidding.

"STEP IN!"

Whereas the focus thus far has been on those who are already in fellowship with Christ but are yet to attain to the level of growth in Him that would make us less prone to yield to the enticements of the world, now our focus will be on the non-believer. The designation of "non-believer" is not unique to those who are presently in this category, for every human has been a non-believer at some point in his or her lifetime. In fact, the text tells us that Moses made a decision to suffer along with the people of God, which means that prior to that, although he was a Hebrew, before identifying with the people of God, he was a non-believer. After Adam, everyone apart from Christ had to make a conscious decision to become a believer in God or not. God, by His grace, gifted us with the capacity to make the right choice, but the decision is up to us. I consider the act of this decision making to be the point of "stepping in." To "step" into the family of God by faith was what Moses was said to have done; it is also what every believer has done; and it is what every non-believer should do.

Keeping in mind that the writer of Hebrews declared that it was by faith that Moses did what he did in saying no to Egypt and yes to God, as we focus on the act of "stepping in," the importance of stressing that it was by faith alone that Moses was able to accomplish that feat should be readily apparent. Again, there was nothing appealing about the predicament of the people of God that could have led Moses to want to take that amazing step. Though they were slaves and were treated inhumanely, he preferred to be identified with them than with their oppressors. He trusted that a life lived for God, even if it meant suffering reproach, was better than all that Egypt had to offer. From the outside looking in, the life of the people of God did not seem like much, but through the eyes of faith he was able to see that it was an abundant life. Though each has its own nuance, the testimony of every child of God is basically the same as Moses' testimony: there came a time when we chose to "step in" by faith. We did not know all the intricacies of the life we were "stepping into," but by faith we trusted that it was the life we needed because God would be our Father; and if God was going to be our Father, we would be in the best family in all creation.

Having now been accepted into the fold, the only regret that anyone who has truly "stepped" into the family of God should have is that they did not do it sooner! The fullness of the joys could not have been known prior to taking the "step" of faith. Now being on the inside, as the apostle Peter put it, we "*rejoice with joy inexpressible and full of glory*" (1 Pet 1:8). The good news is that no one has to remain on the outside and deprive himself or herself of this inheritance. The family of God is open to everyone to join. The Savior Himself promised that He will by no means turn away anyone who comes to Him (John 6:37). The invitation has been extended, but it is up to the individual whether to accept it or reject it.

The Lord promised to give abundant life to all who come to Him (John 10:10); but again, we can never truly understand this unless we take the "step" of faith, so that by definition this "step" has to be by faith. Still, according to the richness of His grace, God does provide unmistakable signs to let those on the outside know that something better is in store for them. Perhaps your world has been falling apart, and although you understand that coming to Christ does not necessarily mean that all of your problems will be solved overnight, you note that in your present state there is no peace. Meanwhile, you know of children of God who appear to have peace on the inside despite being in the midst of similar storms. Or are you tired of carrying the heavy burdens of sin? David, in the Psalm 38, expressed in dramatic terms what this syndrome is like, which every human has felt at some time. We simply were not "constructed" to carry such weight! *"Like a heavy burden they are too heavy for me"* (Ps 38:4). Those were the psalmist's words but I am convinced that many feel the same way today. Others, because they are still blinded by the false pleasures of sin might not yet realize this, but for those of you who are tired, this is an indication that something better is awaiting you.

God so loves you that He makes the necessary effort to surround you with His love to the point that you will want to "step in." And if you are blinded by the present "pleasures" that the world is offering you, have you ever noticed that those things do not bring fulfillment to your life? Perhaps at one point when you enjoyed some of them the pleasure was so intense that you may have thought that those things were the reason for living; but then the next moment reality set in, and you realized that there has to be more to life. Because you fail to accept abundant life, which only comes from God, you continue to strive for more of what the world has to offer, since you need a steady supply of it in order to feel happy. But despite having those things, there remains emptiness on the inside; on the other hand, true joy only comes from God, which lasts and lasts and lasts, and no one can take it away from you!

Finally, even if you are content with the way things currently are in your life, despite your being outside of fellowship with Christ; have you ever thought of what comes next? Have you ever pondered the thought of whether what you now enjoy is all there is to life? I think most would admit to hoping for more. If that is your thinking, then I would liken that admittance to being the equivalent of one of those signs I spoke of concerning God's attempt to convince you that the life He promised to give to those who trust Him is far better than anything you can imagine. God gives these signs to pique your interest; but now you have to take the next step, and by faith do what Moses and many of us have done in "stepping in"! It is now up to you! So please "step in," and by the word of God I assure you, you will never regret taking that "step" of faith!

Principle Nine

Faith is the only means whereby we are justified

"By faith the harlot Rahab did not perish with those who did not believe, when she had received the spies with peace."

Heb 11:31

THE PREVIOUS PRINCIPLE HAS prepared us for the conclusion of an exciting and enlightening journey of display of heroism by many of the champions in the faith in the history of God's people. In the preceding principle we learned that only faith working to mature us can enable us to see beyond the present pleasures of this life, which oppose God's will, and give us the desire to want to live for God. The current principle takes us from the point of the refusal to continue to indulge in the world's pleasures, to being engrafted into the family of God—which is the process of justification.

If one is not justified, none of the previous principles will matter in the end, because when we stand before God the only thing that will matter is whether we have been justified! Since this concept is so important, then, close attention must be given to this principle to ensure that we do whatever is necessary to be counted among those who are justified.

What is justification? For a definition, I quote Unger, who succinctly states, "Justification is a divine act whereby an infinitely Holy God judicially declares a believing sinner to be righteous and acceptable before Him because Christ has borne the sinner's sin on the cross and has become 'to us . . . righteousness' (1 Cor 1:30; Rom 3:24)."[1] There are three key components to this definition which I would like to highlight since understanding them will be vital for the overall understanding of the term. First, it is a divine act of God, which means we are absolutely

---

1. Unger, *Bible Dictionary*, 729.

incapable of obtaining it on our own; there is no human means possible whereby we can enter into fellowship with God. Paul said in Ephesians that this salvation, which we have received and enjoy, is *"not of works, lest anyone should boast"* (Eph 2:9). Understanding this is important because it safeguards us from seeking righteousness by any other means that one might be inclined to engineer, other than through God. Justification is a free gift from God and it cannot be obtained in any other way. The second element of the definition focuses on the end result of justification in that it ensures that we are given a righteous standing before God and are acceptable unto Him. Now there will be times when we might not feel like this is the case but we will need to hold on to the truth that we are indeed acceptable before God. The final facet focuses on how justification was made possible. Yes it is a divine and gracious act of God; but in order for God to provide it, a price had to be paid; and the only price that was sufficient was paid and was accepted by God: the sacrifice of His only Son, Jesus Christ. *"Therefore, having been justified by faith, we have peace with God through our Lord Jesus Christ"* (Rom 5:1).

How amazing is justification? The story of Rahab provides some answers. Despite compressing Rahab's actions into a single verse, the writer of Hebrews did not fail to convey the essence of what she did and what she obtained by doing it—despite her shameful lifestyle. Also, he maintained her infamous title—prostitute. Though the Biblical account does not explicitly state anywhere that Rahab abandoned this lifestyle after her rescue from the destruction of Jericho, one might speculate that it is reasonable to assume that she did, especially in light of her spectacular deliverance and her familiarity with who the Hebrews were and the nature of their God (Josh 2:9–11). It is also possible that the writer of Hebrews may have considered these things but kept the title, not because he wanted to ignore this likelihood in order to convey a debased image of her, but to emphasize the point that it was by faith only that she was justified and not because of anything she had to offer. Furthermore, it should be noted that while in hiding the spies she performed the works of faith, it was faith nonetheless, made complete later by her works, which ultimately justified her. Accordingly, in one short verse, the writer twice makes this same point: first by opening with the assertion that it was by faith that she did not perish, and also by noting that it was because of her faith that she was saved. Only afterwards does he mention her receiving the spies in peace, which was the work that eventually made her faith complete. Faith therefore is the key that opens the door to justification.

Rahab serves as a prototype for others to learn the significance of justification. The theological treatises of many of the writers of Scripture, such as that of the great theologian and apostle, Paul, are all marvelous in explaining this act of God whereby He freed us from sin and shame. But the simple story of Rahab, demonstrates what the process of justification is all about.

Illustrating justification as being a divine act of God, Rahab appealed to the spies to swear to her by the Lord that they would spare her life. In this display of faith she demonstrated her awareness that although she was performing a noble deed in hiding the spies, it was really God's decision, not the spies' or hers, whether or not she should be saved. Rahab recounted the things that the Lord had done to other nations such as Egypt and the two kings of the Amorites (Josh 2:9–10). In doing so, she actually acknowledged that it was God's prerogative to decide who the recipients of justification should be. As a result, she did not simply ask for the spies' promise not to destroy her and her family, but beseeched them to swear by the Lord, knowing that if God was not in the decision, there would be no guarantee of being spared.

In terms of the second aspect of what justification involves: receiving a righteous standing before God and being acceptable unto Him, Rahab clearly received both. Following the defeat and conquest of Jericho, we are told that because of what she did, Rahab was able to dwell in Israel. She was considered to be free of the guilt of her people and accepted into the family of God's people (Josh 6:25). That is justification! Rahab was not treated as an outcast in the Hebrew society, but as one of them; she was engrafted into the family.

Rahab's justification also demonstrates the third key component of justification—Christ's atoning death on the cross as the means whereby one is justified. If we recall the earlier discussion in chapter 8 concerning a theme of the writer of Hebrews, as seen in the telling of both Abraham's and Moses' examples of faith, of putting forth the idea that some looked beyond their time and toward Christ, we can observe this same theme in the example of Rahab, even though in this case the writer does not explicitly state it. That the writer believed that justification is through the sacrificial death of Christ is evident in his arguments about this issue in earlier chapters of the book (Heb 7–10). Keeping this in mind, then, it could be that the writer expected his readers to know that this aspect of Rahab's justification was implied and her forward look by faith toward Christ did not need to be explicitly mentioned as was done in discussing the examples of Abraham and Moses, in which cases it was less apparent how by faith they looked beyond the immediate and unto the eternal.

In every aspect of justification, therefore, Rahab's example serves as a model for what God can do and does for those who, by faith, allow Him to justify them. Although it is a divine act of God, it can only take place with our consent, which is why our having to allow Him is emphasized. Also, if there is to be a genuine gift of justification, the three factors which we just discussed must be evident: it must be wrought by God; we are given a righteous standing in His sight and are accepted into His family; and it is only possible because of the shed blood of Christ. If by faith we have reached out to God in believing that He justifies through Christ, we can have the confidence in knowing that just as we have requested, God has performed!

JUSTIFICATION IS BY FAITH

Faith in God to believe Him to justify the ungodly is absolutely the only means whereby we are justified. There is absolutely nothing that any human being can do to merit this awesome favor of God. God, in His love, provided the means whereby, if we desire to be justified, we can obtain it. As a prototype, Rahab's example of one who obtained justification, illustrates this truth of justification as being only by faith. Because of how it adds great emphasis to this fact, perhaps now it will be appreciated even more why the writer maintained the title of "prostitute" in speaking of Rahab. Since being a harlot was not an esteemed profession even back then in Jericho, it should have been easy to find many who, according to human judgment, were of better moral character than this woman. Nevertheless, none of those so-called "more morally upright than Rahab" survived the destruction, and the only ones who did were Rahab and those whom she interceded for! How could this be that a morally debased person was the only one found worthy to be bestowed this privilege upon and was also the reason why others—her loved ones— were spared? The answer is simple, yet profound; it was because of her faith.

Likewise, not those who are morally upright in their own eyes or in the estimation of humans will be considered to be righteous in God's sight; only those who believe like Rahab did. Just as it was in the city of Jericho when Rahab dwelt there shortly before the city was destroyed, destruction is also looming over our land. The news of it has been proclaimed in every generation by God's messengers, but there is a mixed response. Some, because of having a self-righteous attitude, ignore it. Some have the false notion that they will be admitted into the everlasting kingdom because they are good law-abiding citizens who even go beyond the call of duty of obeying the law to being considerate of their fellow humans in extending a helping hand through various charitable gestures. But while those who commit such acts of kindness are to be commended, the fact remains: they do not meet the criteria for acceptance into the family of God. There is simply only one criterion that qualifies a person for receiving such honor: justification by faith through our Lord Jesus Christ.

As a result of this one doorway to the Father, it is not necessary to provide individual explanations as to why every other proposal leads away from the Father. There is simply not enough money that we can have to suffice, no particular title, no family relationship, no religious belief, or any other thing can substitute to render us worthy of this gift. One exciting implication of this claim is that it causes the playing field to be leveled, thus giving everyone the same opportunity to receive this blessing. So whether it is an uneducated person, the poorest person, a morally debased person, the most notorious criminal, an educated person, the richest person, a good law-abiding citizen, whoever—the opportunity for receiving this grace is the same for all. Imagine what it would have been like if those who are "better off" than others could have obtained the exclusive rights to the "justification market." I picture that scenario as being similar to approaching the gates of an exclusive club but not being able to enter because we do not have the necessary amount of money, connections, skills, education, or other determined qualifications for admission designed to exclude the common folk. But thank God that the eligibility for admittance into the family of God was not determined by any human! God, by His grace, which flows from His love for us, made it so that even the most common person or the one who might be a disgrace to society, is eligible for this gift. In this sense, Rahab thus becomes the model for us in that although she was possibly scorned in Jericho because of her lifestyle, she was not only made eligible for this gift by faith, but received it.

This good news should be comforting to the two types of people that are in the same category as Rahab was. Before noting how, let me clarify that to be considered as being in the same category as she was in does not necessarily mean that all who are in it share in the same behavior as she did in being prostitutes, but it speaks of those whom society may look upon as being shameful and scarred forever. The first type of people are those who think so lowly of themselves that they cannot bring themselves to thinking that God can truly forgive them of their past and then consider them as being righteous in His sight. They are overwhelmed by their past sins, and because of a refusal to allow God to free them, they end up further entrapped in sin where not even God seems able to help them. If that person is reading now, I would like you to know that Rahab, your role model, is one who has been there and has demonstrated successfully that you no longer have to remain in that condition. She set the example of what to do when you have become tired of being in that state. The past must be put behind you because it is something that you simply cannot change! Jesus promised not to reject *anyone* who comes to God through Him (John 6:37). If you reach out by faith to Him and allow Him to help you put your past behind you then justification is most certainly yours.

The other type of person like Rahab are those who, despite their shame, have received and accepted justification by faith, yet still continue to struggle with the enormous guilt and shame that resulted from their past deeds. To obtain an insight into just how haunting this can be, one simply has to look at the life of the great apostle Paul, as told in the book of Acts and in his own writings. In reading both sources, it should be observed that even following years in Christ's service, he still lamented and struggled to come to grips with the horrible acts of violence and antagonism which he inflicted upon the church of Christ (see, for example, Acts 22:19–20; 1 Cor 15:8–9 ; 1 Tim 1:12–14). Although he knew and confessed that Christ had forgiven him, the images could not be erased from his mind. Perhaps even as late as his last days he may have thought about his consent to the stoning of Stephen, and the fact that those who did it placed their clothing at his feet as he stood close by; he may have thought about those whom he threw into prison for preaching the gospel, as well as countless others who were fearful of him; of the many families that he tore apart; and perhaps other memories that we cannot imagine.

This same syndrome of guilt and shame continues to plague many of God's people today. We understand that God casts our sins into the depths of the sea (Mic 7:19); but because reminders are ever before us to take us back to those moments when we committed such acts and cause us to reflect on the harmful effects they may have caused others and ourselves, we find it difficult to put them behind us and move on. Furthermore, the issue is even more compounded when others are aware of those actions. Whenever the thought of moving forward comes to mind, we remember that others know about our former ways, and we think they will doubt that there is genuine change when they see us try to move on. In addition, there is the constant whispering into our spirits by the enemy of our souls to try to instill doubt that God can truly liberate from our past. All in all, the memory of our foolish ways of the past can be stifling to our forward progress into the bright future that God has for us. This is a reality that is being experienced by many in the body of Christ. Nevertheless, to the one who desires to be freed from it, it can be accomplished by faith in Christ.

Justification by faith does not only consist of the judicial act whereby we are forgiven and placed into a peaceful standing with God—but also God's act to move us into a peaceful standing with ourselves! God is by no means in the business of making us at peace with Him while desiring that we remain at war within ourselves. Rather, His will is for us to be able to stand in His presence without shame, as well as to be able to look at our image, both in a physical mirror and in the mirrors of our minds, and be able to smile at what we see, which is a new creation (2 Cor 5:17)! We can be confident that God does not want to see His children's heads hung down in the shame of their past, which is why when we come to Him He puts our past behind us and makes all things new. Instead of hanging our heads down in disgrace, therefore, let us allow the Lord to lift us up in thanksgiving for His grace, because He is the One who lifts up our heads (Ps 3:3).

While it is true that where our standing is concerned, the Lord does indeed only see us as being clothed in the righteousness of Christ and not in the filthy garments of our past foolishness, if we are going to be able to put those things behind us it will require that we believe that God has indeed forgiven us. If we do this, it should also follow that if we believe that God, the One whom we ultimately offended and who had the right to condemn us, has forgiven us, we should also forgive ourselves. Remember, provision for being able to be at peace with ourselves has been made in the gift of justification, but we need to accept it. Unless we suffer amnesia, the memory of the past will always remain with us; but God can cause us so to forgive ourselves that we learn to function as if we forgot the past.

Thereafter, any thought of those things can be processed positively in that they will serve as lessons to teach us how better to conduct ourselves—and we can also use them as testimony to warn others, lest they make the same mistakes as we made.

As an example, while the apostle Paul could not erase the memory of his past, he clearly appeared to understand and accept by faith that he was justified and absolved of the guilt and penalty of his former ways. The evidence of this is in the confessions he made to the same such as, *"But by the grace of God I am what I am, and His grace toward me was not in vain . . ."* (1 Cor 15:10); and, *"And the grace of our Lord was exceedingly abundant, with faith and love which are in Christ Jesus. This is a faithful saying and worthy of all acceptance, that Christ Jesus came into the world to save sinners, of whom I am chief"* (1 Tim 1:14–15). These statements sound like those of one who was confident that he was pardoned; and though he appeared to look back in regret from time to time, wishing he had not acted the way he did, he obviously was able to function to the full capacity that God expected of him. In fact, the remainder of the verse quoted above from 1 Cor 15:10, and the next verse after the quotation from 1Tim 1:15, both confirm this. In them the apostle went on to say that he labored more than his peers who did not have as horrible a past as he did (1 Cor 15:10), and that his efforts became a pattern for others who would later believe in Christ (1 Tim 1:16).

What Paul experienced was not unique to him, but God intends for everyone to experience the same, upon being justified. Note that Rahab could not erase her past or her memory of shameful things she had done, yet being able to move on was something she could learn to do and in all likelihood she was successful in doing. While we are not given any further details of her life in Scripture following the conquest, except that she dwelled in Israel after Jericho had been destroyed, we do know that if she was determined to change her former lifestyle and allow it to remain in the rubble of Jericho, she had to learn to forgive herself as God had already done. This was what the apostle Paul had to learn, what Rahab had to learn, and what we must learn today as well. Understandably, whenever others who are familiar with our shameful past remind us of it, we might not feel like we have been justified during those moments. Also, even when only we know of such past, the shame within can be overwhelming and cause us not to feel justified, as we consider how debased our actions were. Nevertheless, at such moments, we must remember that we were not called to rely on feelings—but on faith in the promises of the word of God that let us know that we have been justified!

In responding, therefore, to those who might question our justification, to argue will not be necessary, but to simply follow Paul's example by responding, "*. . . by the grace of God I am what I am*" (1 Cor 15:10). And that is—justified! We should appeal to the promises in God's word and allow that initial work of justification to continue to work in us so that both skeptics and critics, even if they never admit seeing a genuine change in us, will eventually have nothing more to accuse us of besides our past. If they choose to do so, we can find consolation in the fact that by the simple virtue of their inability to raise any valid accusations against us following the day of our salvation, it is an ultimate admission to the witness of a change in us, since there is nothing to accuse us of from that point forward. Also, when the condemnation comes from within we must remember that *"if our heart condemns us, God is greater than our heart, and knows all things"* (1 John 3:20). Our hearts do not have the last word on whether we are forgiven or not. God has the last word, and He promises to forgive us if we, by faith, confess our sins and repent of our evil ways.

Comprehending the implications of justification by faith are therefore very important if we are going to be able to walk in the victory that God secured for us. We understand that faith is the key that unlocks the application of justification in our lives to free us from our sins. Justification is available, but we must believe and trust God to receive it. Faith is also the substance that gives us the confidence to believe that we have indeed been accepted into the family of God, upon being justified. Because we have not entered into heaven as yet, our confidence for knowing that we have been grafted into the family of God can only come by faith, seeing we continue to reside on earth despite having heavenly citizenship. Finally, we can be confident in knowing that we have been delivered from the wrath to come.

ULTIMATE BENEFIT
OF PUTTING REAL FAITH INTO ACTION

As we prepare to come to the end of this exciting journey of the demonstration of real faith being put into action, I think it is fitting that we take some time to discuss this very important event that is sure to come in our future. This event is the destruction of the world as we now see it, including everything in it. From Scripture, we understand that this devastating act of God is necessary because of sin and the effects it has caused. These effects are not limited to our planet earth, but they impact the entire universe. Everything God created in the beginning was good, but when humanity sinned, everything in the universe was adversely affected. This is why the apostle Paul said the whole of creation is eagerly awaiting our redemption (Rom 8:19–23). The ultimate fulfillment of this redemption can only take place at that time when there is a thorough purging of sin, which means that all those who practice sin will be eternally confined to a place of punishment called hell, and this world that has been tainted with sin must be destroyed so that a new earth and new heavens can take its place (2 Pet 3:10–13).

Now the story of the destruction of Jericho and Rahab's place in it should serve as an example for us today with respect to this eventual and imminent destruction. The news of impending destruction was evidently widespread in Jericho because Rahab testified to this fact in her report to the spies when she spoke about the nation's fear of the Hebrews and their God (Josh 2:9–11). The only problem was that everyone else besides her and her loved ones trusted in other means for survival rather than salvation from God. For Rahab, survival did not depend on her obedience to the king of Jericho, or anything else—but on faith that if she put her trust in God and positioned herself on God's side, she would be spared of the approaching destruction. Likewise, the word has been proclaimed in every generation, warning of coming judgment and destruction; still, many trust in alternate means, other than justification through Christ's atoning death, for deliverance. Some trust in their moral and ethical standards, their charitable deeds, and various religious beliefs that contradict Scripture. They fail to realize that only those who, like Rahab, believe in the One who alone can deliver them through the only God-ordained means—the acceptable sacrifice of His dear Son, Jesus the Christ—will be saved.

By trusting in God to justify us, we exercise faith to believe that through justification, we will be saved from the coming wrath. Accordingly, just like Rahab who, by faith, believed in advance that she would be spared whenever Jericho was overrun, we can also be confident even now by faith that whenever destruction comes upon the land, we will be spared. And not only that, even if we should die before the rapture—the moment of actual physical rescue—takes place, we can depart this life with that same confidence by faith that we will not be condemned on the day of judgment. In this respect, we can identify with Joseph who gave instructions concerning his bones just before he died. By faith he was confident that, at the appointed time of rescue, his remains would be taken to the land of Canaan; and although that set time would not be for another 400 years, when it arrived, his faith was honored. His faith and hope, therefore, were symbolic of what ours should be upon our departure from this life; although much more exciting, for while his hope in death was for his bones eventually to be carried to the land of promise, our hope in death is eventually to be raised to life again and to be with Christ forever! Thus, the ultimate fulfillment of receiving the things that we hope for by faith, which is to dwell in Christ's presence forever, will be finally realized. This was our ultimate hope when we were justified by faith, and by faith we will receive it! *"Now faith is the substance of things hoped for, the evidence of things not seen."*

Amen.

Conclusion

A Prayer from my Heart

I THANK YOU, LORD, for the illumination that has come as a result of this journey through the principles, which were demonstrated by some of the past heroes in the faith. I pray that others will be inspired to put similar faith into action as those witnesses displayed. I do realize that this is not the end of the journey. The journey has only just begun, because this was by no means an exhaustive list of all of the principles of faith. The writer of Hebrews admitted, when he concluded the roll call, "*And what more shall I say? For the time would fail me to tell of Gideon and Barak and Samson . . .*" (Heb 11:32). I too am aware that there are other principles that you desire for us to understand. In the meantime though, please help us begin with these and allow them to inspire unfeigned, bold, and even radical faith in us, as we strive to serve you wholeheartedly. By faith as we do so and mature, I ask that you reveal more principles that will take us to higher levels of faith and maturity in you.

Finally, Lord, I ask that you help us to be more mindful of those who are rejecting your plan of justification that you provided to ensure that we would be spared from coming destruction; and even more importantly, to guarantee our obtaining eternal life in sweet fellowship with you. Help those of us who believe to be even more vigilant than we have been before in seeking you for inspiration to demonstrate real faith in our lives. May our witness to the unsaved be so convincing and overwhelming that it leads them to you, so that in the end both they and we will rejoice together, and you will be glorified. Lord, I thank you by faith for hearing this prayer, and attending unto this plea.

Amen!

Bibliography

Birch, Bruce C. "The First and Second Books of Samuel." In *The New Interpreter's Bible: A Commentary in Twelve Volumes*, edited by Leander E. Keck et al., 2:947–1383. Nashville, TN: Abingdon Press, 1998.

Craddock, Fred B. "The Letter to the Hebrews." In *The New Interpreter's Bible: A Commentary in Twelve Volumes*, edited by Leander E. Keck et al., 12:1–173. Nashville, TN: Abingdon Press, 1998.

Fretheim, Terence E. "The Book of Genesis." In *The New Interpreter's Bible: A Commentary in Twelve Volumes*, edited by Leander E. Keck et al., 1:319–674. Nashville, TN: Abingdon Press, 1994.

———. *The Pentateuch*. Nashville, TN: Abingdon Press, 1996.

Grenz, Stanley, J. *Theology for the Community of God*. Grand Rapids, MI: Wm. B. Eerdmans Publishing; Vancouver, BC: Regent College Publishing, 2000.

Johnson, Luke Timothy. "The Letter of James." In *The New Interpreter's Bible: A Commentary in Twelve Volumes*, edited by Leander E. Keck et al., 12:175–225. Nashville, TN: Abingdon Press, 1998.

King Jr., Martin Luther. "I See the Promised Land." No pages. Online: http://www.mlkonline.net/video-martin-luther-king-last-speech.html.

———. "The I Have a Dream Speech." No pages. Online: http://www.usconstitution.net/dream.html.

Mann, Thomas W. *The Book of the Torah: The Narrative Integrity of the Pentateuch*. Atlanta, GA: John Knox Press, 1988.

Unger, Merrill F. *The New Unger's Bible Dictionary*, edited by R. K. Harrison et al. Chicago, IL: Moody Press, 1988.

Wiles, Virginia. *Making Sense of Paul: A Basic Introduction to Pauline Theology*. Peabody, MA: Hendrickson Publishers, 2000.

Willis, Wallis, "Swing Low, Sweet Chariot." No pages. Online: http://www.bookrags.com/wiki/Swing_Low%2C_Sweet_Chariot#History.htm.

Wood, Leon J. *A Survey of Israel's History*. Revised ed. Revised by David O'Brien. Grand Rapids, MI: Zondervan Publishing House, 1986.

Zodhiates, Spiros. *The Complete Word Study Dictionary: New Testament*. Chattanooga, TN: AMG Publishers, 1992.

www.ingramcontent.com/pod-product-compliance
Lightning Source LLC
Chambersburg PA
CBHW072149160426
43197CB00012B/2311